锦绣中华

Let the World Know More About China

China, an ancient country with a long history and brilliant civilization, has a vast territory with magnificent great mountains and big rivers as well as rich tourist resources. For years, I have long been looking for the way which attracts more people in the world to know about our country and nation. During my trip to Europe in 1985, I visited the famous Madurodam "Lilliputian Land" in Holland when an idea came to me and I was thinking how great it would be if we could build a miniature scenic spot in which China's renowned scenic attractions and historical sites could be concentratedly displayed so that people could admire and know more about China's beautiful scenic wonders, splendid history and culture as well as various national customs and habits in a shorter time. What I thought then won the support from my fellow-travellers. In autumn 1985, approved by the State Council, China Travel Service (Holdings) H.K. Ltd. was responsible for the exploitation and construction of Overseas Chinese Town, an area of 5 square kilometres, and we immediately decided to invest and build "Splendid China" Miniature Scenic Spot in Overseas Chinese Town. Through three years' planning and hard work, we have overcome all sorts of difficulties. In the course of practice, our plan has been gradually accepted by people. The miniature scenic spot which reflects China's ancient culture and history as well as rich tourist resources has now appeared before your eyes at last.

"Splendid China", is the crystallization of collective wisdom as well as the embodiment of collective willpower, perseverance and the spirit of cooperation. It has won the great support from various places of the country and good cooperation from many experts, professors, engineers and technicians. Here, I would like to take this opportunity to express our heartfelt thanks and highest respects to personalities of various circles who have ever made their contributions to the building of "Splendid China".

"Splendid China" has, to some extent, expressed the characteristics of Chinese nation — diligence, courage and wisdom. It also reflects the pride of our great nation and will deepen the love of the decendants of Huangdi for our great motherland and cherish a deep affection for the Chinese nation.

"Splendid China" is a window of China's history, culture and tourist resources. It will make the world know more about China, arouse the interest of tourists from various countries to visit China, bring about a great advance in China's tourist industry, and thus promote mutual understanding and friendship between the peoples of China and other countries in the world.

"Splendid China" is an exploration in the development of China's special tour. We sincerely hope you will give us your valuable comments and suggestions.

(Ma Chi Man)

Vice-Chairman & General Manager of China Travel Service (Holdings) H.K. Ltd.
General Manager of China Travel Service (H.K.) Ltd.
Director of Shenzhen SEZ Overseas Chinese Town Construction Headquarters

A Brief Introduction to "Splendi

"Splendid China", with all its charm and distinctive style, emerging at the picturesque Shenzhen Bay, is a unique tourist attraction featuring miniatures of the best known scenic spots of China. It excels its counterparts in China and the world, in area, in the amount of sceneries reproduced and in the fullness of the nation's culture, art, history and ancient architecture reflected therein. It has a strong appeal to the visitors all over the world to come and admire this charming sight.

"Splendid China", situated at Overseas Chinese Town in Shenzhen Special Economic Zone, is jointly invested and built by China Travel Service (H.K.) Ltd. and Shenzhen SEZ Overseas Chinese Town Economic Development Company.

The conception of "Splendid China" was put forward by Mr Ma Chi Man, General Manager of China Travel Service (Holdings) H.K. Ltd. in 1985, who, in the light of the development in international tourism, and the consideration of China's vast territory and rich tourist resources and also the advantage of Shenzhen being adjacent to Hong Kong, suggested to build a miniature scenic spot in which China's renowned scenic beauty and historic interest can be concentratedly shown. With this miniature scenic spot as a "window", China's brilliant culture and long history will be further popularized and give more people of the world better understanding of China, and thus promote the friendly contacts between the peoples of China and other countries and give great impetus to the development of China's tourism.

Early in 1986, a meeting was specially held, soon afterwards, the overall plan of "Splendid China" began in 1986. Based on the suggestions of experts and scholars from China and abroad, the overall layout, the choice of places for scenic spots, the scale of scenes and the materials to be used were repeatedly discussed, constant improvement and replenishment of the content were made for the plan and in September 1987, the breaking ground of scenic area started. For the reappearance of the style and the artistic value of the genuine scenic spots and historical sites, most of the miniature replicas were jointly built up by the local cultural relics research department and ancient building unit in charge of construction. Among them, there are more than one hundred contemporary China's first-class ancient-building experts, carving artists, horticulturists, acting as technical advisors or joining the work themselves. Over two thousand engineers and technicians from around twenty provinces, cities (districts) of the country, thousands of li away, made a special trip to Shenzhen, braving the wind and dew, seeking from best to excellence. It took only about two years to finish seventy-four scenic spots and other basic, complete sets of facilities in the first phase of the project, and it was open to visitors in September 1989. The second phase of project has begun, and the scenery buildings such as the Summer Palace in Beijing, the Imperial Garden in the Imperial Palace, the Town God's Temple in Shanghai, the Temple of Goddess of

hina" Miniature Scenic Spot

the Sea in Fujian, Tengwang Tower in Jiangxi, the Twin Pagodas in Liaoning, etc. are under construction.

Occupying an area of 30 hectares, "Splendid China" is three times larger than Taoyan "Lilliputian Land" in Taiwan and twenty times larger than Pattaya "Lilliputian Land" in Thailand and Madurodam "Lilliputian Land" in Holland as well. After the whole project being completed, the number of scenic spots will reach over one hundred. The first batch to be opened for public is seventy-four. Most of the tourist attractions are reproduced on the scale of 1:15, some are 1:10 or 1:8, the largest one is 1:1. It is different from what is done in other country's "Lilliputian Land", at which the scale is 1:25. As every single brick and tile is strictly miniatured and reproduced according to the scale of the originals, so the lifelike, miniature reproductions in "Splendid China" excel other counterparts which are only seeking the outer resemblance. "Splendid China" Miniature Scenic Spot has, so to speak, its unique artistic features in conception, the scale of construction or the natural sceneries and the mould of figurines. Each scenic attraction is a remarkable piece of work of art.

The eighty scenic spots and historical sites opened in "Splendid China" are arranged scientifically according to the location of China's real scenic places. They can be classified into three categories: ancient buildings, scenery with rivers and mountains, folk customs and local dwelling. Ancient building group includes palaces, monasteries, temples, towers, pagodas, bridges, etc. which are too numerous to be counted; scenery with rivers and mountains group comprises famous high mountains and big rivers, grotesque peaks and queer rocks while folk customs and local dwelling group reflects the different styles of buildings and houses, habits and customs of this multinational country. You can have a look at 50,000 Lilliputian lifelike pottery figurines in "Splendid China" and get a good idea of traditional habits and customs of different nationalities in China. For example, you can enjoy the grand spectacles of the "Wedding Ceremony of Emperor Guang Xu" in Imperial Palace, "Holding a Memorial Ceremony for Confucius" in Confucius' Temple. You may also get a view of various festive activities, such as dance, wrestling, archery, horse race, etc. on the Mongolian grassland.

Tourists can go to Comprehensive Service Area in the southwest of "Splendid China" and walk into "A Street in Suzhou" to buy some handicraft arts, local specialities or have a taste of traditional flavour of delicacies and snacks from various places of the country, or enjoy the performance of traditional folk songs and dances, and the 360 degree giant-screen film showing the magnificent, graceful land of China.

As is spoken by people, visiting "Splendid China" means seeing round the ancient, civilized country with a history of 5,000 years, and travelling over a land of charm and beauty only in one day.

CON

ENTS

Ancient Buildings

China, an ancient, civilized country with a history of 5,000 years, has rich, splendid cultural relics and historic sites. In 1958 and 1982, the State Council announced there are 5,634 government-protected cultural sites in the whole country. Among them, the major ones are 242, such as the site of the ancient man, the imperial capitals and ancient cities, imperial palaces and tombs, ancient buildings and projects, ancient bridges and towers, ancient temples and pagodas, grotesques and steles, residences of famous persons, gardens and parks, unearthed artifacts, etc. still dazzling brightness to this day. They are the pride of the Chinese nation, and have a strong appeal to visitors of various places of the world to come here one after another.

The Great Wall

The world-famous Great Wall was built in 475 B.C. After the unification of China by Emperor Qin Shihuang, he began to link together the great walls of various states built in the Warring States Period (475-221 B.C.) and thus it became the greatest military defensive construction in the world. The Great Wall at present was mainly built on the basis of the great wall of the Ming Dynasty, so it was also called "Ming Great Wall". Starting from Shanhaiguan Pass in the east and ending at Jiayuguan Pass in the west, the Great Wall has an approximate length of 6,700 km. With a history of more than 2,000 years, it ranks among one of the world's eight wonders.

The Great Wall in Splendid China, with a total length of 1,000 metres, is designed and constructed by experts and professors of China Great Wall Association. It begins from "the bank of Yalu River" in the east and ends at "Jiayuguan Pass" in the west (built on the replica of ancient Great Wall). According to the different historical periods, this Great Wall was built in three parts: the first part was built in the Spring and Autumn Period (770-476 B.C.), using the materials of cobble stones. The second part was built with dolomite. As the wall had undergone many changes and damaged by wind and rain, it weathered to yellow white. The third part was built with bricks, which are the same size as dominoes. These bricks are made according to the "real bricks" on the scale of 1:10. The small bricks are transported from Beijing in far distance for the building of the wall, then laid piece by piece. One worker can only lay an area of half a metre square of the wall each day, and six million small bricks are used in all.

The Great Wall is the symbol of Splendid China. You can admire the majestic, magnificent Great Wall from various places in the scenery park.

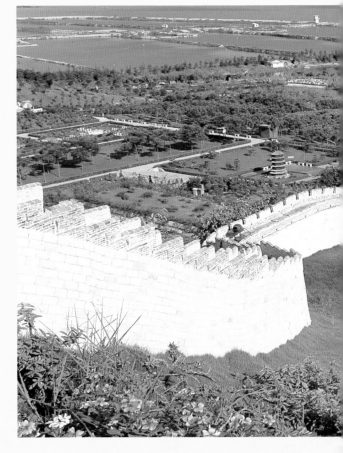

The Imperial Palace

he Imperial Palace, also known as Forbidden City, Palace Museum as well as Old Palace, was built between 1406 and 1420 or the 4th-18th years of the reign of Emperor Yong Le in Ming Dynasty. The whole architectural group occupies an area of 720,000 square metres, with floor space of 150,000 square metres and over 9,000 rooms. It is the largest and most complete group of ancient buildings standing in the world.

The Imperial Palace has its main entrance, called the Meridien Gate (Wumen), on which are built five phoenix towers, soaring high into the air. It was here that the emperor annually announced the new calendar, presided over military ceremonies and confirmed and annulled death sentences. Behind the Meridien Gate, five golden water bridges, exquisitely carved, span the shimmering inner Golden Water River. The Gate of Supreme Harmony (Taihemen) in the north of Golden Water Bridge is the main gate of the Hall of Supreme Harmony (Taihedian), the Hall of Central Harmony (Zhonghedian) and the Hall of Preserving Harmony (Baohedian). This is the largest gate in the Imperial Palace.

The three halls at the outer palace stand eight metres above the ground on three-tiered terrace of white marble. The whole construction is compactly laid out, full of power and grandeur. The Hall of Supreme Harmony in the south, 64 metres wide, 37 metres long and 27 metres high, with painted eaves, golden decoration and vermilion columns, is the most magnificent and resplendent of the palace complex. The throne in the hall decorated with gilt gold and carved jade is flanked by six columns with a diameter of one metre each, entwined with golden dragons. High above the throne is a coffered ceiling with gilded designs of dragons toying with pearls. They ingeniously match well. This hall was named the "Hall of Golden Throne" where grand ceremonies were held.

The Hall of Central Harmony is the place where the emperors rehearsed for ceremonies. To the north of it is the Hall of Preserving Harmony in which banquets and imperial examinations were held. The wooden structure in the hall and the colour paintings on the inner eaves are the originals in the years of Wan Li in Ming Dynasty.

The miniature replica in front of the Hall of Supreme Harmony is the reappearance of the grand spectacle of the "Wedding Ceremony of Emperor Guang Xu", showing the emperor's life of complicated etiquette, solemn atmosphere as well as extravagance and waste.

The Imperial Palace in Splendid China is reproduced according to the Imperial Palace in Beijing on the scale of 1:15. For resembling the real objects, 35,000 pieces of goldleaf, equal to 647 grams of gold, have been used in the building of Imperial Palace and the Temple of Heaven. For the reappearance of the grand spectacle of the "Wedding Ceremony of Emperor Guang Xu", about one thousand pottery figurines are made and arranged in the place. Their attractive appearance and facial expression are really true to life, and there are innumerable variations of forms with unique artistic style.

Tian An Men

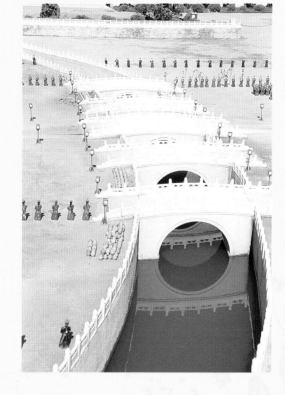

T ian An Men, also called the Gate of Heavenly Peace, and the Imperial Palace were built simultaneously. With a history of over five centuries, imposingly standing in the south of the Imperial Palace, it is the great masterpiece of the brilliant culture of the Chinese nation as well as the symbol of New China.

Tian An Men, 37 metres high, consists of huge white marble base, brick red walls and gate towers. The towers and the palace walls link up together as a whole, and the double-eaved, yellow, glazed tiles give it a majestic and magnificent look. The spacious great hall in it, 58 metres wide, has 36 windows on all sides decorated with exquisite, crimson carvings of rhombus patterns. It appears commodious, simple and unsophisticated, solemn and dignified. In front of the gate, a pair of ornamental pillars erect on both sides, soaring straight up into the sky. A pair of lifelike white marble lions, raising their heads with fixed gazing and awe-inspiring are guarding on both sides of the gate. The outer Golden River flows on in front of the gate, the carved white marble balusters linking up one after another like white ribbons and five outer Golden Water Bridges like dragons lying between the river banks.

The majestic and magnificent rostrum, the imposing and impressive ornamental pillars, the pretty and mighty stone lions, the refined and graceful river and bridges all make the shape of Tian An Men look more solemn and dignified with a taste of primitive simplicity, beauty and charm.

During the Ming and Qing Dynasties, Tian An Men was the place where large-scale national celebrations were held. Formerly emperors let down imperial edicts from the top of the gate in a gilded box to kneeling officials, and common people were not allowed to enter it. But, nowadays, Tian An Men decorated in rich and gay colours is open to warmly welcome the tourists from various places of China and the world.

Tian An Men in Splendid China is reproduced on the scale of 1:15. The Golden Water River under the gate and the beautifully carved five white marble Golden Water Bridges spanning over the river, the two vigorous stone lions and the imposing ornamental pillars matched up skilfully show that Tian An Men is a building complex with perfect art of architecture.

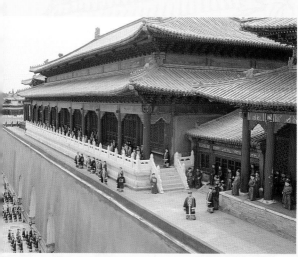

The Temple of Heaven

The Temple of Heaven was built during the 4th year of the reign of the Ming Emperor Yong Le, occupying a total area of 273 hectares, three times as big as the Imperial Palace. It is the place where the emperors of Ming and Qing Dynasties worshipped heaven and prayed for good harvests. Its design is very much related with heaven, full of imagination and romantic colouring.

The Temple of Heaven is divided by two walls into outside temple and inside temple. The southern parts of the surrounding walls are square while the northern parts are semi-circular. This symbolizes the ancient belief that heaven was round and the earth square. The Temple of Heaven is the general name for Circular Mound Altar and the Hall of Prayer for Good Harvest. Entering the western gate of the temple to the right, there is a path which leads through the trees to the Hall of Abstinence. The Hall is a group of buildings surrounded by a square enclosure and a moat. Continuing along the entrance path, you can come to a raised passage called the Red Stairway Bridge. This broad walk connects the two sets of main buildings in the Temple of Heaven enclosure. Turning northward and entering through the Gate of Prayer for Good Harvest, one will see the Hall of Prayer for Good Harvest in its full grandeur. It is a lofty cone-shaped structure with triple eaves and a blue-tiled roof. The entire structure is 123ft. (37.5m.) high and is supported by twenty-eight massive wooden pillars, each of which symbolizes a different thing. The four central columns, called the "Dragon-Well Pillars," represent the four seasons. Surrounding these four, there are two rings of twelve columns each, the inner ring symbolizing the twelve months, and the outer ring, the twelve divisions of day and night. The centre of the stone-paved floor is a round marble slab which has a natural pattern of dragon and phoenix. The whole building is a wooden structure joined together by means of wooden bars, laths, and brackets without the use of any iron or bronze.

The Hall of Prayer for Good Harvest serves as the place where the emperors prayed for good harvest every year on the fifteenth day of the first moon by the lunar calendar. Behind this Hall is the Hall of Heavenly Emperor, a place to keep the tablet of heaven and other divine symbols during the year. Going back out through the Gate of Prayer for Good Harvest and proceeding southward, you can visit the Imperial Vault of Heaven and the Circular Mound Altar.

The Circular Mound Altar is the place for making offering to heaven on the winter solstice. In ancient China the odd numbers (1,3,7,9) were regarded as "sun numbers". So the number of stone slabs in any parts of this Altar (terrace floor, staircases, and balustrades) is made in multiples of 9. After the ceremony, the tablet of the God of Heaven and tablets of the Gods of Wind, Rain, Thunder, and Lightning were brought back to be stored in the Imperial Vault of Heaven.

The surrounding wall of the Imperial Vault of Heaven and the centre stones of the Circular Mound Altar produce a strange acoustic effect. People can make "telephone calls" through the wall. Two people standing behind the side chambers, one on each side, and speaking softly to the wall, the voice may be heard by each other. This is often referred to as Echo Wall. If you stand in the centre of the upper terrace of the Circular Mound Altar in front of the three large rectangular stones and shout, you will hear echo unusually loud. These are called the Triple Sound Stones.

The Temple of Heaven in Splendid China is reproduced on the scale of 1:15. For resembling the real object, 35,000 pieces of goldleaf, equal to 647 grams of gold, are used in the building of the Temple of Heaven and the Imperial Palace. For the sake of the reappearance of the grand spectacle of the "Ritual of Emperor Worshipping the Heaven and Praying for Good Harvest", hundreds of pottery figurines are especially made and arranged here. Their attractive appearances and facial expression are really true to life, and there are innumerable variations of forms and unique artistic style.

The summer Palace

The Summer Palace, an imperial palace of Qing Dynasty, originally called Qingyu Garden, is a famous scenic spot in Beijing. It covers an area of more than 4,000 mu and three fourths of it is occupied by water.

In 1888, by the order of the Empress Dowager Cixi, funds for the modernization of navy were used to reconstruct and refurbish more than 3,000 palaces, galleries and pavilions in the garden and changed its name into "Yiheyuan". The Summer Palace, 20 km from Xizhimen Street contains Wanshou Shan (the Longevity Hill) and Kunming Lake. Visitors cannot fail to be impressed by the greenery of the hill and the clear blue lake at its foot. Ascending from a magnificent arch by the side of the lake, one will pass Paiyun Gate, Paiyun Palace, Tehfei Palace and then further uphill to reach the summit of Wanshou Shan — the Hall of Buddhist Incense and the Temple of Sea of Wisdom. On the top of the hill, you can have a bird's-eye view of the picturesque landscape. Inside the garden, there are the Spring Showing Pavilion, the Long Corridor, the Garden of Harmonious Interests, the Marble Boat, the Seventeen Arches Bridge, the Jade Belt Bridge, etc. They have a variety of artistic styles, and each has its own unique features. The pagoda on the Jade Spring Hill and the West Hill with peaks rising one after another blend harmoniously, forming a unified, resplendent landscape.

The Summer Palace in Splendid China is reproduced on the scale of 1:15. The magnificent structures and lovely scenes make the Summer Palace look more beautiful and attractive.

Royal Garden in Imperial Palace

 ocated in the north of Imperial Palace, with an area of 18 mu, Royal Garden was called "Gonghouyuan" in Ming Dynasty, meaning "a garden behind the imperial palace". It was the place where emperors, queens and concubines had relaxations or entertained themselves.

A huge bronze incense burner cast in the years of Emperor Qianlong's reign in Qing Dynasty stands at the centre of the garden with flowers in a riot of colours. Two 500-year-old cypresses crossing each other form an arched door. A pair of stone dragons spurt sparkling, crystal water. Duixiu Mountain is green and luxuriant. The artificial hills built with stones from Lake Tai, Lizhao Hall with the collection of a large number of rare books and halls, terraces, lake-side pavilions in various kinds of styles as well as numerous potted-landscapes in four seasons, all these make the garden rich in poetic flavour and full of vitality.

What impresses tourists most is the paths among the bushes which are built with pebbles of various colours, and this kind of layout is rarely seen in the building of imperial garden.

The Royal Garden in Imperial Palace in Splendid China is reproduced on the scale of 1:15. With the outstanding feature and beautiful shape, the garden has its own unique artistic style among other royal gardens.

Yuanmingyuan Garden

uanmingyuan Garden, the most magnificent, exquisite royal garden in the period of great prosperity of Qing Dynasty. It has carried forward the fine tradition of royal garden of China in more than 3,000 years and absorbed the landscapes of southern China and the cream of royal garden and ingeniously merged with the distinguishing feature of western-style architecture, hence its name "the garden of all gardens".

Unfortunately, this world-famous garden was looted and burned down by the Anglo-French joined forces in 1860, and now has become the ruins. In the past 100 years, people have come to visit and pondered on the past in front of the ruins of this renowed garden, showing their concern for the culture of human history and angrily condemning the barbarous crime committed by the imperialists.

For the reappearance of this magnificent garden of the times, Shenzhen Splendid China Development Co., Ltd. has built "Yuanmingyuan Miniature Scenic Spot" in "Splendid China Theme Park". Occupying an area of more than 20,000m², the company has invested over Rmb 30 million and built some chosen attractions, such as Peace for All-China, Unviersal Peace, A Wonderland on Fanghu Island, Dashui Fa, Haiyan Banquet Hall, The

Shell Carving in Xieqi Bei, Wanhua Maze, Fuhai Sea and An Immortal Abode on Penglai Island on the scale of 1:8, besides, the ruins of the column of Western-style Building was reproduced on the scale of 1:1, which comprehensively shows the history of prosperity and decline of the Yuanmingyuan Garden. In this scenic place, the traditional Chinese architecture and western-style architecture are skilfully combined together. The period of building "Yuanmingyuan" once again showed the cultural exchange between China and the West.

In this scenic area, a model of the full view of Yuanmingyuan is also shown with the advanced technique of the combination of sound and light, so that it can vividly show the splendid times of Yuanmingyuan and the sight of the Yuanmingyuan burned by the Anglo-French joined forces.

At present, the garden is being built in full swing and is scheduled for completion by the end of 1994. The reproduction of Yuanmingyuan has historical and realistic significance of developing the culture of Chinese nation, carrying out the education of patriotism as well as enriching and making the tourism of "Splendid China" more flourishing.

The Ming Tombs

The world-famous Ming Tombs is the place where 13 emperors of the Ming Dynasty (1368-1644) were buried. The tombs are scattered over a basin of approximately 40 square kilometres in area. At its extreme south, there is a huge white marble gate, with six pillars and eleven chambers. The six big pillars of white marbles are all 14 metres high, with relief sculptures of dragons and beasts, showing the royal air, full of power and grandeur. Through the gateway, one can see the Great Palace Gate, or called Great Red Gate. Inside the gate is a wide path called Sacred Way, which is leading to different sites of the tombs, with either side of stone statues and stone animals. The twelve stone mandarin statues are four ministers, four generals, four royal members. There are twenty-four large white marble animals, twelve facing pairs, equidistantly placed on either side of the road in standing and kneeling positions. Six animals are: two mythical animals, lions, elephants, camels and horses. Each is sculptured out of a single rock. The technique is superb and the images are true to life.

In the north of the stone statues, behind the Chamber of Dragon and Phoenix is Chang Ling, the tomb of Zhu Di, the third emperor of Ming Dynasty. This tomb is the largest, consisting of Ling Men Gate, Ling En Gate, Ling En Hall, Ming Lou Building and Bao Cheng Hall. With a double roof of glazed yellow tiles and red walls, Ling En Hall is entirely built of nanmu wood. Among the 60 huge pillars in the hall, the biggest ones are the four standing in the centre, 14.3 metres high, and 1.17 metres in diameter each. To present day, the pillars are neither rotten nor decayed and have a heavy fragrance. This is the only precious art work of its kind in the ancient wooden structures of China.

The Ming Tombs in Splendid China is reproduced according to the original one in Beijing. The number and the image of the stone statues and stone animals are the same as the genuine ones and made of real white marbles on the scale of 1:15 in unique artistic style.

Jin Gang Bao Zuo Pagoda

 in Gang Bao Zuo Pagoda in Dazhengjiao Temple, situated at Xizhimenwai in Beijing, is unique in style, ingeniously conceived and imbued with strong foreign flavour. It was built with reference to the prototype of Bodhikaye Pagoda in India.

In the years of Yong Le in Ming Dynasty, Bandida, an Indian senior monk, went to the court and presented five gold Buddhas and the model of Bodhikaye Pagoda. In order to provide a place for Bandida to spread Buddhism, Emperor Zhu Di himself selected the site and ordered his men to build Dazhengjiao Temple. Before long, Zhu Di died, Emperor Xiao Zong of Ming Dynasty ascended the throne. For realizing the ancestor's good will, he ordered the artisans to fit up the palace and build Jin Gang Bao Zuo Pagoda. The earliest Jin Gang Bao Zuo Pagoda was thus built here.

The square pagoda base, called throne, is 7.7 metres high. The throne is divided into five floors, on the walls of each floor, stone pillars are used to separate the place into groups of niches. There are exquisite Buddhist images and the designs of Buddhist theme engraved in them. At the front and back of the base are opened arched doors, and there are stairs inside spiralling up and leading to the top of it. At the centre and four corners of the base stand five square multi-eaves small pagodas. The biggest one, over 8 metres high with 13 layers, stands in the centre, while the four smaller ones, 7 odd metres with 11 layers each, stand at the four corners. Besides, in front of the pagoda is built a glazed-tile pavilion in the characteristics of Buddhism of China.

The whole pagoda is made of hundreds of pieces of white marble which are carved in advance, glittering and clean. The pagoda is honest and steady in style, compact and of good proportion in structure. The Chinese traditional sculptures and reliefs are found all over the walls of the base and the five small pagodas. With a strong style of Indian Buddhist pagoda and sharp Chinese national design and technique, it is the most complete, preserved Jin Gang Bao Zuo Pagoda among the five existing ones in China.

Jin Gang Bao Zuo Pagoda in Splendid China is reproduced on the scale of 1:15. Unique in shape, ingeniously conceived, the pagoda has various kinds of decorative patterns and designs, Buddhist images and arhats, the reliefs of subduing dragons and tigers carved in superb skill everywhere on the walls of it.

Lugou

Bridge

huge dragon lies between the river banks breathing under the twilight moon and sparse stars.'' Arriving at the bridge at dawn when the rippling water shimmered under the pale moon, Emperor Qian Long of Qing Dynasty was fascinated by the scene and wrote, ''The Morning Moon at Lugou Bridge''. A pavilion with a tablet bearing the inscription in his calligraphy still stands at the east of the bridge. And this formed the origin of the world-famous Lugou Bridge, one of the eight famous scenic spots in Beijing area.

Started to be built in 1189, and completed 4 years later, Lugou Bridge is 266.5 metres long, 7.5 metres wide, and has 11 arches. It is a big and multi-arch bridge with unique characteristics. Worn by wind and rain through more than 800 years and damaged by the war, the bridge still magnificently stretches over the Yongding River nowadays, showing the unusual creativity of the Chinese nation. It was here that the curtain rose on the Chinese people's great war of resistance against Japanese aggression in 1937 with what is known as the ''Lugou Bridge Incident of July 7''. Lugou Bridge is a magnificent ancient structure as well as a famous memorial place of revolution.

The most marvellous thing of the famous Lugou Bridge is the 485 small stone lions. Its stone balustrades have 140 sculptured balusters on either side with a lion carved on the top of each, each lion different in posture from the others. Intriguing are the lion cubs, from a few millimetres to a dozen millimetres in size, playing around the main lion figure, clinging to her breast, crouching at her feet, peeking from behind her ears or squatting on her shoulders. Marco Polo, the famous Italian tourist coming to China in the 14th century, wrote in his travel notes, ''Over the river, there is an extremely beautiful stone bridge. Come to think of it, it is indeed the most wonderful and unique bridge in the world....''.

The Lugou Bridge in Splendid China is reproduced on the scale of 1:15 to the real one over the Yongding River at Guang'anmenwai Street, Fengtai District in Beijing. The 485 lifelike stone lions with various shapes are carved on the 140 balusters on either side of the bridge, full of vim and vigour, innocent and lovely. It may be rated as the acme of perfection.

The White Pagoda at Miaoying Temple

he White Pagoda at Miaoying Temple is the earliest Lamaist pagoda of its kind as well as the most outstanding building of Lamaist pagodas in China. This white pagoda started to be built in the years of the reign of Kublai Khan and completed in the 8th year of his reign in Yuan Dynasty (A.D. 1271). It took eight years altogether. The project is huge and mammoth.

The huge pagoda, two-storey brick building in octagonal shape, 8 metres high, is majestic and splendid. The big Buddhist lotus throne is built at the bottom to support the cylindrical pagoda body which is wide in upper part and narrow in lower part. The pagoda is full and round, bold and unconstrained, like a huge inverted pottery bowl. The body of the pagoda composes of the wheel signs which are linked together by two-layer small thrones, 13 layers in all. Each layer becomes contracted as it goes upward and they are called "Thirteen Days". The round bronze cover with a diameter of 10 metres covers the top of the pagoda. Around it, there hang colourful tassels and 36 bronze bells. When the wind blows, the tassels are fluttering and the bells sounding in clear melody. At the top of the pagoda is placed a small gilded, bronze Lamaist pagoda, 5 metres high and 40 tons in weight.

Anige, a Nepalese architect and designer was invited by Kublai Khan, the founder of Yuan Dynasty to engage in the design and construction of the pagoda. Making reference to Lamaist pagoda in Nepal, Anige completed his masterpiece named the White Pagoda at Miaoying Temple.

The White Pagoda at Miaoying Temple is completely white and looks elegant, solemn and magnificent. It is of good proportion in structure, graceful in line and exquisite in workmanship. From whatever directions you look, the posture of the pagoda is so harmonious that you will be fascinated by its charm of art.

The White Pagoda at Miaoying Temple in Splendid China reproduced on the scale of 1:15, is beautifully shaped, completely white and unique in style.

haozhou Bridge is located at Zhaoxian county, called Zhaozhou in ancient times, hence the name Zhaozhou Bridge. It is also called Big Stone Bridge in the locality. The bridge was designed and built by the famous mason Li Chun at the beginning of Sui Dynasty (A.D.605). It is a single-opening arch bridge spanning the river from south to north. The bridge is 64.4 metres long, 9 metres wide and made of 28 separate rows of stones laid in parallel series and has the characteristics of a mild curve and wide span. There are two small arches at each side of the big arch. The design is aimed at reducing the resistance of the rapid flow and lightening the load on the arch and the foundation. The bridge shows a very high level in design and artistic layout. It is the earliest single-opening arch bridge in the world as well as a masterpiece in the history of bridge architecture.

The bridge, large in size, firm and solid in structure, magnificent in appearance, is really a marvellous creation. During the long years, the bridge has undergone the earthquakes for eight times and wars, great and small for eleven times, and withstood the erosion of water, rain, wind and snow for more than a thousand years. This ancient bridge still erects proudly to this day. Du Deyuan, the famous poet in Song Dynasty once wrote a poem, eulogizing this bridge. There are also poems in praise of the bridge spreading among the folks, for example, the song and dance drama ''A Child Cowherd'', expressing the admiration to the masons who built the bridge.

The Zhaozhou Bridge in Splendid China is reproduced on the scale of 1:15. Owing to the characteristics of a mild curve and wide span, extremely difficult in design, exquisite carvings on both sides of the wall fence and pillars, it creates a unique style of its own.

Zhaozhou Bridge

Imperial Mountain Resort

he Imperial Mountain Resort in Rehe, Hebei province, was also the Imperial Temporary Dwelling Palace of the emperors of Qing Dynasty. It has picturesque scenery and pleasant weather. The resort, began to be built in 1701 (the 40th year of the reign of the Emperor Kang Xi, Qing Dynasty), covers a total area of 5.6 million square kilometres. The whole palace is enclosed by a wall over 10 kilometres long. The gate opens at the southern end of the palace wall. Just inside is the Principal Palace, silent and elegant. This is the place where emperors spent his summer while dealing with the state affairs. The main structure takes its name from the fine-grained fragrant hardwood of which it is built, called Nanmu Hall which is austere and magnificent, using only grey bricks and tiles.

To the southeast of the mountain resort is the lake area. These lakes are interconnected. Pavilions and towers dot the many islets which are linked by causeways. Along the north bank, halls, mid-water pavilions, towers and pagodas are in the style of the architecture of southern China. In the west of the lake are artificial hills with numerous stone caves. When climbing up the top of the mountains, magnificent buildings and towers appear before your eyes.

The Imperial Mountain Resort in Splendid China is reproduced on the scale of 1:15, according to the one in Chengde city, Hebei. The whole construction has its own unique characteristics.

Ancient Star-Observatory

A small town called Gaocheng or Yangcheng in ancient times is located 15 miles away in the southeast of Dengfeng county, Henan province. It is said that in the early years of Zhou Dynasty (3,000 B.C.), the famous politician Zhou Gong Dan once set up a platform to survey the moving of the sun here, the city thus gained the fame. In the 11th year of Kai Yuan in Tang Dynasty (A.D. 723), the local officer set up a stone platform with the inscriptions in memory of Zhou Gong who had surveyed and drawn the moving of the sun in this place. Guo Shoujing (A.D. 279) the famous astronomer in Yuan Dynasty set up 27 observatories in the whole country and this one was the centre of them. This observatory centre, 20 metres north of the platform where Zhou Gong watched the sun, was not named then. In the years of Jia Jing in Ming Dynasty, when Zhou Gong Temple was rebuilt, a tablet of 《 Zhou Gong Temple Doctrine 》 was set up. In the inscriptions, the place named after Ancient Star-Observatory was mentioned for the first time and has been so called until now.

The main part of the star observatory is an inverted-funnel-shaped brick platform and sky measuring scale.

The brick platform is 9.46 metres high, the upper part 8 metres wide in each side and the bottom part 16 metres long in each side. At the centre of the observatory wall is a vertical gap from the top to the bottom. The bottom of the gap is connected with the exquisitely designed sky measuring scale. At both sides of the observatory walls, there are zigzag stairs leading to the top of it. The star observatory is scientifically designed, formed by the straight line and right angles. All is in good proportion, edges and corners clearly demarcated, simple and unadorned in style.

The effect of the star observatory is done by means of the surveying point which is formed by the sky measuring scale and the gap of the platform wall to measure the length of the sun shade and then count them separately and find out the difference in summer and winter, the high and low latitudes and the length of tropical year. This is the earliest observatory building in China.

The Ancient Star-Observatory in Splendid China, reproduced on the scale of 1:15, is exquisite in shape, a mixed structure of brick platform, a square surface as well as simple, unadorned and unique in style.

Longmen Grottoes

ongmen Grottoes are situated at both banks of Yihe River, 13 kilometres south of Luoyang, Henan. The mountainous scenery of Longmen is consistently ranked as the champion among the eight main sceneries of Luoyang. A poet, Li Yuxi in Tang Dynasty composed a poem to praise the beautiful scenery of the Yihe River banks where the grottoes are located. The grottoes, measuring at the height of 1,000 kilometres, are reputed as the cultural and artistic treasure in the world. Longmen Grottoes, together with Dunhuang Grottoes in Gansu and Yungang Grottoes in Shanxi, are the three largest grottoes in China.

Longmen Grottoes were carved at the period of Tai Huo, Northern Wei Dynasty (A.D. 477-499) up to the first year of Guang Fa, Tang Dynasty (A.D. 898) for over 400 years. The grottoes consist of 1,352 caves and 750 niches, housing 100,000 Buddhist statues and images as well as 40 Buddhist pagodas. The highest Buddhist statue measures at the height of over 17 metres whereas the smallest one only of 5 centimetres. The rich collection of exquisite statues and over 3,600 pieces of inscriptions engraved on stone walls or stone tablets provide an important sources for the study of Chinese calligraphy and ancient history of China.

Fengxian Temple, measuring 36 metres from south to north and 41 metres from east to west, is the largest open air niche in Longmen Grottoes. It consists of 9 Buddhist statues of Losona, Disciple, Bodhisattva, Heavenly King, Celestial Guardian, etc. The statue of Losona, 17.14 metres high, is the largest Buddhist statue in the niche. The plump and smooth-faced Buddhist statue has thin and long eyes and brows, expression calm and composed, eyes reserved, with its mouth corner slightly tilting up, showing radiance of kindness and wisdom. Along two sides, the Buddhas are arrayed harmoniously and in well proportion and its shapes are really true to life. Among the statues, Kasyapa is strict and prudent, Anunda, pious and meek, Bodhisattva, solemn and reserved. Heavenly King, brows knitted and eyes glaring and Guardian powerful and robust. The statues, whose varied shapes and expressions are so skillfully carved that it can be rated as the representative work of the sculptural arts in Tang Dynasty.

The Longmen Grottoes Buddhist Statue in Splendid China is reproduced on the scale of 1:3. The lively and vivid shape of the statue creates an artistically rich and colourful image. Its posture is so graceful and its expression so elegant that it is acclaimed as the acme of perfection.

Yungang Grottoes

 ungang Grottoes, located at the southern cliffs of Wuzhou Hill in Datong city of Shanxi province and stretching one kilometre long from east to west, were excavated according to the structure of the mountain. They are known as one of the three major cave complexes in China and also the world-famous treasure house. They were first built in the third year of Xing An during the reign of Emperor Wen Cheng in Northern Wei Dynasty (A.D. 453) and nearly completed in the nineteenth year of the reign of Emperor Tai He (A.D. 495) before the capital removed to Luoyang. The construction of the carved stone statues extended to the era of Zheng Guang (A.D. 520-525), accomplishing 53 grottoes with a total number of 51,000 stone statues. It is recorded in Shui Jing Zhu (Commentary on Waterways Classic A.D. 466-527) that the scene of excavating the grottoes was majestic and full of grandeur.

Yungang Grottoes are so rich in content and exquisite in sculpture that they not only hold a prime position in the artistic history in China but also the essence between the eastern and western cultural exchange. The initially carved caves from the sixteenth to the twentieth are known as the "Five Caves of Xian Yao", completely majoring in the construction of Buddha statues. The stone statues, giant in size, are carved in the style of primitive simplicity and vigour to exhibit majesty and power hence religious flavour is prominently outstanding in these stone sculptures in the early years.

Situated in the middle part of the group of grottoes are the fifth and sixth grottoes which are noted for their rich variety. Its beauty and magnificence seep out from its peculiarity and the skillful and different ways in carvings. Besides, strong flavour of daily life is permeated. It naturally reminds people to think of the flourishing and prosperity of Buddhism in those years, hence they become the most unique masterpiece of the Yungang Grottoes.

The huge Buddha, sitting on the lotus throne, is the outstanding feature in the centre of the fifth grotto and is also the largest one among the Buddha statues in Yungang Grottoes. It measures 17 metres high, 15.8 metres wide, sitting cross-legged, each at 4.65 metres long. Carved reliefs with Buddhist inscriptions cover four sides of the walls manifesting a majestic and solemn environment.

The sixth grotto is in the height of 6 metres, large-scale in shape and thick with carvings. At the central part of the rear chamber stand the 15-metre-high square pillar and 2,000 pieces of stone carvings of Buddhist statues, Bodhisattvas, arhats and flying apsarases in various sizes which are the focus of all attention. Among them the "Fozhuantu" which depicts the life story of Sakyamuni, the founder of Buddhism, is especially distinctive. Once you stay inside, you seem as if you placed yourself in the realm of Buddhism, fascinating and interesting.

Yungang Grottoes in Splendid China are reproduced on the scale of 1:3. The image of "Sanshifo", majestic and magnificent, captures one's attention. Stone sculptures of Bodhisattvas, arhats and flying apsarases are vivid, multifarious and varied in forms exhibiting a unique style of its own.

Shaolin Temple

Shaolin Temple, located at the northern foot of Mount Shaoshi of Songshan Mountain Range in Henan province, was built in the reign of Emperor Wendi in Northern Wei Dynasty (A.D. 495). Shaolin means the forest of Shaoshi Mountain. Some main buildings are seen here. Daxiong Hall (Hall of the Great Buddha) looks grand and magnificent, with colourful paintings, various forms of reliefs, solemn Buddhist statues, smoke curling up and full of religious atmosphere. Tianwang (Heavenly King) Hall stands elegantly and gracefully, with carved beams and painted rafters. The four Heavenly Kings stretch their chests with glaring eyes and majestic looking. The Abbot's Room, resplendent and serene, is the dwelling place where the abbot lived and handled daily affairs since various dynasties in the past. It is said that Emperor Qianlong of Qing Dynasty once lodged here and wrote poems in praise of this place. Behind it is Lixue Pavilion, also called Damo Pavilion. A bronze statue of Damo is worshipped in it. According to the legend, in A.D. 527, Damo, an Indian monk, reached here by crossing the sea and began to propagate the Law of Chan School in China. He enrolled monks and disciples to practise martial arts for self-defence. Ever since then, Shaolin Temple was called "Home of the Founder" of Buddhism in China. At the beginning of Tang Dynasty, in the battle against Wang Shichong, Li Shimin, Emperor Taizong of Tang Dynasty, was rescued by the monks of Shaolin Temple. Therefore he cited the monks for their meritorious deeds and the temple gained the reputation of "Number One Temple under Heaven". Shaolin kung-fu or Shaolinquan became famous at home and abroad. The story of "thirteen monks rescued the emperor of Tang Dynasty" spreads far and wide. The monks of Shaolin Temple practised martial arts very hard, famed for its combination of interior mildness and exterior vigour as well as superb skill. The traces of the then monks' practising kung-fu are still somewhat visible. There remained a practising pit on the brick floor. It is said that it was formed due to long-term treading when the monks stood on the ground, exerting their forces, or made straight leaps in the practice in "Pile-standing". The marks can also be found on the walls of Buddha Halls. With its consummate fighting skills and great martial feats, handing down a good reputation to present day as well as far-reaching influence, Shaolinquan or Shaolin boxing enjoys high reputation in the world.

Shaolin Temple in Splendid China is reproduced on the scale of 1:15. It preserves the solemn atmosphere of religion. The characterization of the figures of 500 famous arhats in Shaolin Temple is in unique artistic style, different facial features, bold and vigorous lines, animated and lifelike in varying gesture.

The Pagoda in Songyue Temple

The pagoda stands at the southern foot of Songshan Mountain in Henan province, hence the name Songyue Temple Pagoda. Songyue Temple, started to be built in the second year of Shen Gui during the reign of Emperor Xiao Ming in Northern Wei Dynasty (A.D. 519), was completed in the following year. At present, the Songyue Temple is already in a state of decay, but Songyue Temple Pagoda is perfectly in good condition. It boasts the earliest multi-eaved, ancient brick pagoda now existent in China.

It is constructed in brick walls and hollow in the centre. The design of the pagoda is free from worldly cares, showing great ingenuity and originality. It is the only pagoda in China with the shape of dodecagon at the exterior. The main part of the pagoda is in the form of regular octagon. The width of the outer base of the pagoda is 10.6 metres in diameter, the inner base 7.6 metres and the height of the pagoda is 41 metres. The whole pagoda is clearly divided into upper and lower parts. The lower part takes up one third of the structure. There are four doors opened on it, facing south, east, north and west. The doors are decorated with circular arches on their tops. The other eight sides of the walls are decorated with corner columns in bold and vigorous lines and carved brick lions of primitive simplicity. The upper part consists of 15 layers with multi-eaved roofs. There are 492 small windows on the short walls between the eaves of the pagoda and most of them are fake ones, simply for the sake of decoration. Among them, only ten windows on the seventh layer are genuine and used for the natural lighting of the upper part and thus creating a peculiar effect of sunlight coming in through the top. Above 15 multi-eaved layers is the top composed of lotus thrones, seven-tier rhombus wheel signs and the round decorative "pearl" as its summit. The eaves of the pagoda become contracted layer by layer as they go upwards and form the parabola contour of hardness touched with softness.

The upper part of the pagoda is crimson and magnificent. The carved brackets supporting the eaves are ingenious and full of variety. The lower part is white, plain and bright. The carvings and decorations are of primitive simplicity, bold and unsophisticated. The whole huge pagoda looks delicate and pretty, dignified and elegant as well as bold and graceful. This is the very typical style of architecture in Northern Wei Dynasty.

Going up Songshan Mountain, you should, naturally, climb up the highest peak of the Central Mountain, Junji Peak, rising 1,494 metres above sea level. You can have the whole view in a far distance, the peaks of the endless mountains shrouded in mist and clouds rising one behind the other. Ouyang Xiu, the famous poet of Song Dynasty once wrote a poem with five characters to a line depicting this marvellous view of steep precipices and cliffs covered with a sea of clouds, faintly visible. It is no doubt that the peak has been reputed by many men of letters as "towering aloft in the skies and piercing halfway into the heaven" since ancient times. Even the Emperor Qian Long of Qing Dynasty did it just the same. When he came to "Junji Peak", he was bound up with affection for the charming scene and couldn't help himself write a poem and set up stone tablets.

Songyue Temple Pagoda in Splendid China is reproduced on the scale of 1:15. To make the miniature scene picturesque and true to life, the beautiful environment surrounded by mountains is assiduously created to achieve its perfection.

To the west of Shaolin Temple, there is a place between slopes and mountain valleys with picturesque scenery and serene environment, where a number of pagodas are scattered among the green trees and it is indeed a splendid sight. This is the well-known Pagoda Forest of Shaolin Temple. Each pagoda has the remains of a senior monk of Shaolin buried in it. The first pagoda was built in the year of 791 and the last one was built in 1803, the 8th year of the reign of Jia Qing in Qing Dynasty. So far 240-odd pagodas are preserved either in brick or stone. Among them, two pagodas were built in Tang Dynasty, three in Song Dynasty, six in Jin Dynasty, forty in Yuan Dynasty, and the rest of them were built in Ming and Qing Dynasties. It is the biggest pagoda forest in China and a natural museum of ancient pagodas built in various dynasties of China as well.

The shapes of the pagodas are varied and complicated. They are different in style, a blending of the ancient and the modern, tall and short, big and small, unequal and irregular. It has a seven-storey huge pagoda in 14.6 metres high or a one-storey, small and exquisite pagoda in 1 metre high. Varieties of sculptures and artistic decorations are engraved on the pagodas, adding infinite queerness and wonder to it. If you place yourself in the midst of the pagoda forest, you will be dazzled and cannot take it all in.

There are two entirely different pagodas in the pagoda forest, which are the historical evidence of the exchange of Buddhism between Sino-Japan and Sino-India and of the friendship between peoples of these countries. In the east of the pagoda forest is the Ju An Pagoda for Abbot, which was built in 1339, in the years of Hui Zhong's reign in Yuan Dynasty. At the back wall of this pagoda, the inscription composed by the celebrated Japanese monk Shoogen was engraved on it. In the west is the pagoda for Monk Jiu Gong Tian Zhu, which was built in 1564 during the years of Jia Qing in Ming Dynasty. In April 1973, when visiting the pagoda forest, Guo Moruo the famous poet and scholar, eulogized Shoogen's inscription, which was depicting the long-standing friendship between the peoples of China and Japan as well as China and India. The Pagoda Forest in Splendid China is reproduced according to 240-odd pagodas in Shaolin Temple in various shapes and different styles, tall and short, big and small, bearing unique characteristics.

The Pagoda Forest

akyamuni Pagoda is also known as Yingxian Wooden Pagoda. As the name implies, it is a pagoda purely of wooden structure as well as the highest and the oldest wooden pagoda extant today in China. It started to be built in A.D. 1056 and it assumes an important guardian post in the Fogong Temple in Yingxian county, Shanxi province.

This five-storey pagoda with six eaves is octagonal in shape. With the inner hidden storeys included, it can be considered as having nine storeys. Each upturned tier of eaves is brightly painted with exquisitely carved beams and painted brackets like rosy clouds encircling the pagoda. The outline of the diamond-shaped summit of the pagoda which measures 14 metres high exhibits a vigorous appearance. When it is in combination with the elegant iron Buddhist temple, it possesses a natural grace and solemn outlook. It shows not only majesty and magnificence but it also owns a tall and graceful bearing.

The opening of the lower tier of the pagoda faces to the south and its centre is hollow. There are wooden stairs leading to the top of the pagoda. From the second tier above, every tier is constructed with upturned terrace and corridor with guarded fence. From here, tourists can have a wide view of the picturesque surroundings when climbing to the top of the pagoda.

An eleven-metre high Sakyamuni statue gilded in gold, is seated right in the centre of the Buddhist Hall at the lower tier. There are corridors in between pillars providing a thoroughfare for worshippers to pay religious homage to the Buddha. Whenever there is Buddhist service held here, there is a scene of smoke curling up and the big cymbals playing in unison against the glittering of the candle light and the golden shine of the Buddha statue, light and shade in turn, hence creating a solemn and mysterious space with thick religious atmosphere.

The Yingxian Wooden Pagoda in Splendid China is reproduced on the scale of 1:15. The whole pagoda is of wooden structure, antique and quaint in style.

Yingxian Wooden Pagoda

Confucius (latinised form of Kong Qiu or Kong Zi), the founder of the Confucian School, was the well-known politician, thinker and educator in the end of the Spring and Autumn Period. Confucius' Temple, Confucius' Mansion and Confucius' Forest, the three precious sites of Confucius, called "Three Kongs", are the gems of Qi and Lu States.

In 478 B.C. (the year following the death of Confucius), Duke Ai of Lu State ordered that Confucius' old house with three rooms be turned into a temple. After repeated renovation and expansion in ensuing dynasties (beginning from Western Han Dynasty), the temple has now become a group of ancient buildings. At the length of one kilometre from south to north, it covers an area of 22 hectares, surrounded by tall red walls. The temple is composed of nine courtyards with 466 halls. The main buildings symmetrically aligned along the north-south axis are Dacheng Hall, Hall of Sleeping, Sage Exhibition Hall, Kuiwen Pavilion, the Thirteen Stone Tablets, Apricot Terrace, etc.

Covering an area of 1,800 square metres, about 25 metres high, Dacheng Hall is the main palace where sacrifices were offered to the great sage. This double-eaved roof and nine-spine building has crisscrossed brackets, yellow tiles and vermilion window frames. The 10 stone columns at the front, measuring 6 metres high, one metre in diameter, are carved in relief. Each of them has a pair of twisting dragons playing a ball round it and being set off by mountain peaks, billowing waves and scudding clouds; they are superb masterpieces of ancient stone carving. The hall is decorated beautifully but still retains its solemnness, resplendent and splendid. It can match each other with "Hall of Golden Throne" in the former Imperial Palace in magnificence and is ranked among the three best ancient buildings of China.

In the northernmost of the temple is the Sage Exhibition Hall. Up to 120 pieces of pictures are drawn and words carved on the inner walls inside the hall which record the main activities of Confucius and it is also the exhibition of Confucius' life story, which has high artistic as well as historical value.

Kuiwen Pavilion, in front of Dacheng Hall, is a Book-Store Building for storing the books given by emperors in ensuing dynasties. Kuiwen Pavilion, a big building made of wood, 23.35 metres high, has three rows of upturned eaves, four systems of brackets inserted between the top of the columns and crossbeams. The structure, of classic elegance and magnificence, exquisite and solid, stands firm after experiencing earthquakes for many times. It is really a miracle in the history of ancient architecture.

The Confucius' Temple in Splendid China is reproduced on the scale of 1:15. In the "Memorial Ceremony for Confucius" are arranged more than 2,000 lifelike, mini figurines with unique artistic features and a variety of forms.

The Temple of Confucius

Nine-Dragon Screen

In 1392, Zhu Gui the thirteenth son of Emperor Zhu Yuanzhang who was the first emperor of Ming Dynasty, was granted the title of Prince in Datong county, Shansi province. In building the mansion of Prince, he built the Nine-Dragon Screen as the wall facing the gate of the house. The mansion was unfortunately destroyed in the war at the end of Ming Dynasty leaving Nine-Dragon Screen safe and sound until now.

The length of Nine-Dragon Screen is 45.5 metres from north to south, 8 metres high and more than 2 metres thick. The base made of blue and green glaze is 3 metres high and its upper part is a relief sculptures of 41 pairs of dragons, each pair playing with a pearl. In the lower parts, there are 75 pieces of colour glaze with the sculptures of oxen, horses, sheep, elephants, dogs, rabbits, deers, lions, unicorn, flying horses and so on. Covering the top of the walls is the system of grace brackets, with the relief sculptures of art.

The main part of the screen is 3.73 metres high on which there are nine dragons made of 426 pieces of colour glaze, the nine dragons are flying and dancing in the sea of clouds, vivid and energetic. The yellow dragon, sitting in the middle, facing the south with the body stretching out, and the tail winding right, is the chief dragon. On both sides of it are a light yellow dragon or yellow dragon and purple dragon, yellow alternating with green jade in pairs. Some are sitting and gazing fixedly, some plunging into the sea, some jumping to the sky and others crawling forward swiftly. The whole composition is lovely, the colour impressive and the posture vigorous and graceful.

In front of the dragon screen is a pool, its water clear and blue. When the breeze blows, the water is rippling. The inverted images of the nine dragons reflecting in the water are rising and turning. One will wonder if real dragons are swimming and dancing in the park.

The Nine Dragon Screen in Splendid China is reproduced on the scale of 1:4. The whole composition and the colour match very well, and the nine dragons soaring in the sky and dancing in the sea of clouds are really true to life.

Feihong Pagoda

uangsheng Temple, located on Huoshan Mountain in Hongdong county, Shanxi, is a group of Buddhist temples renowned in China for its long-standing history and the variety of precious cultural relics. Embellished with old, verdant cypresses and clear, limpid rivers, the whole area looks more beautiful and picturesque. Feihong Pagoda, initially built in the first year of Huan Huo's reign in Eastern Han Dynasty (A.D. 147) and standing loftily on the peak of beautiful Huoshan Mountain surrounded by green cypresses, is the gem of the ancient architecture in Guangsheng Temple.

Feihong Pagoda is the largest and the best preserved glazed pagoda in China. It was built simultaneously with Guangshen Temple but underwent repeated renovations and repairs. The existing pagoda was built during the years of Zheng De and Jia Jing in Ming Dynasty (A.D. 1515 to 1527). In the 34th year of Kang Xi's reign in Qing Dynasty (A.D. 1695), Lin Fen Basin suffered the earthquake of 8 magnitude. It was a miracle that Feihong Pagoda was safe and sound except the inscriptions on the top of the pagoda sustained a slight damage.

Octagonal in shape, this thirteen-storey pagoda measures over 47 metres high. It is hollow in the middle with an ingeniously designed spiral staircase which is rarely seen. The thirteen-tier eaves of the pagoda diminish inwardly at each tier while the outlook of the upturned eaves is bold and vigorous but of well proportion. The pagoda, laid with green bricks, is covered with shining yellow, green and blue tiles, gleaming with dazzling brightness and radiance. In between the upturned eaves of the lower three tiers, they are decorated with the brackets inserting into columns and crossbeams, prisms, images of Buddha, Bodhisattvas, Buddha warriors, attendants, dragons and tigers, rare birds and animals as well as peculiar flowers and plants which are all glazed whereas thousands of carvings in relief and hanging sculptures are extremely splendid and superb beyond compare. Among them, the figures, vivid and lively, are in various postures with no resemblance to each other completely manifesting wonderfulness and ingenuity.

The artisans' high craftsmanship is fully shown by their delicate selection of tiles in different shades of colours matched with the wooden winding corridors of exquisite styles. When the whole view is set off against the backdrop of the blue sky without a wisp of cloud, the pagoda, gleaming in the sunshine, seems to be colourfully decorated with the gorgeous and rosy clouds like a dancing rainbow, hence the name Feihong Pagoda (Flying Rainbow Pagoda).

Feihong Pagoda in Splendid China is reproduced on the scale of 1:15. Its structure retains the artistic style of Yuan Dynasty. The expressions and postures of the pottery myths in the frescoes all around are lifelike and really true to life. Thus, it is acclaimed as the masterpiece in the painted sculpture.

43

The Midair Temple

"**T**he fairy temples are built on the cliffs, covered up by white clouds time and again." A group of hanging temples appearing like the richly decorated jade palaces gently descending from the sky are found jutting out from the rock cliff of Cui Ping Peak in the valley of Hengshan Mountain in Hunyuan, Shanxi. This is the Midair Temple, uniquely charming and is the number one among the eighteen sceneries in Hengshan Mountain.

The Midair Temple was first built at the later stage of Northern Wei Dynasty and underwent constant reconstructions in Jin, Yuan, Ming and Qing Dynasties but no great changes were made to its form. The existing buildings and palaces numbering forty in all are hanging on the cliff, their height irregular and strewn here and there. The layout of the complex is reasonable and one can see variations in symmetry and connection in scattering.

A stone tablet in the temple presents a detailed account of how the temple was rebuilt and how an artisan surnamed Zhang undertook this arduous task despite other workers' retreat in face of difficulties. Some of the component parts had been made beforehand and he led other workmen to make a detour to Cui Ping Peak. They let down the workmen together with the building materials with ropes from the top of the cliff. For several years, they worked high up on the air, hammering and chiselling out grottoes to inlay the supporting beams and pillars until they completed this renovation project.

The Midair Temple is propped up slantingly by the horizontal beams and vertical pillars which are stuck into the rock. The workmanship is so excellent that such a firm and solid structure is still safely hanging on the cliff nowadays in spite of the precarious weather of wind and rain as well as scorching sun or repeated strong earthquakes in many centuries.

The composition of the temple is somewhat peculiar comprising Taoist "San Gong Hall" and also Buddhist "San Sheng Hall". Inside "San Jiao Hall" are the statues of the founders of Buddhism, Taoism and Confucianism. The founder of Buddhism, Sakyamuni is seated in the middle whereas to the right is Confucius, originator of Confucianism and to the left is Laozi, founder of Taoism. This is a way symbolizing the feudal and cultural structure of three religions mingling into one.

The Midair Temple in Splendid China is reproduced on the scale of 1:15. In order to attain the authenticity to the real object, range upon range of "high mountains" are built rising one behind the other. Then, a group of temples are slantingly propped up by the horizontal beams and vertical pillars. From the distance, the temples are built ascendingly against the mountain ridges. Taking a close look of the view, one realizes that it is the superb masterpiece of the Midair Temple.

Nanchan Temple

anchan Temple is located at two sides of the Lis Village. People do not know when it started to be built. Only in Great Buddha Hall, there is an inscription which says that the temple was rebuilt in the third year of Jian Zhong under the reign of Emperor De Zong in Tang Dynasty. It is the earliest wooden structure existing in China at present.

Nanchan Temple faces south. The main buildings in the temple are the gate, east and west side halls and the Great Buddha Hall forming a compound in the style of quadrangle. Apart from the Great Buddha Hall built in Tang Dynasty, the rest were rebuilt in Ming and Qing Dynasties.

The Great Buddha Hall, a complete wooden structure, is a typical architecture of Tang Dynasty, showing the strong Tang's style of art. It is a building with the design of single-eave roof, mild turnings, flying eaves and in good proportion. The hall looks magnificent in form. Without a single column in the hall, it adopts the methods of piling up eaves pillars and layer upon layer of brackets inserted between the tops of eaves pillars and cross beams to support the roof. The sections of the materials are rational and the joints firm and secure vertically and horizontally,

succinct in structure, a skilful integration of mechanics and aesthetics and ingeniously conceived. It is majestic, simple and unsophisticated, harmonious and beautiful. Its interior joints are solid and firm, and best quality in materials. Since the Great Buddha Hall was rebuilt, it has undergone earthsquake of magnitude 5 for eight times, yet it is not damaged at all. It shows the superb technique of architecture in the middle period of Tang Dynasty.

In the Great Buddha Hall, there still preserves 17 Buddhist clay statues. Apart from those found in Dunhuang Grottoes, these coloured clay statues are the precious ones in China.

The wooden structures built before Tang Dynasty in China were damaged and almost found nowhere. Nanchan Temple is the only wooden structure of Tang Dynasty which is perfectly preserved to this day. It has not only high artistic value, but is also a valuable example in the study of wooden structure in Tang Dynasty.

The Nanchan Temple in Splendid China is reproduced on the scale of 1:15. The modelling of the roof beams is succinct in structure, the brackets are piled up on the tops of the eaves pillars to support the roof and no column in the hall. It has the artistic style of Tang Dynasty.

Jin Ancestral Temple

in Ancestral Temple is located at the fountain-head of the Jin River at the foothill of Mount Xuanweng, southwest of Taiyuan, Shanxi. The temple was built in memory of Tan Shuyu, the second son of the founder of the State of Jin, Emperor Zhou Wu, hence it is also known as Tan Shuyu Temple. Its initial time of construction cannot be traced. But dating back as far as 1,500 years ago, it was recorded in Shui Jing Zhu (Commentary on Waterways Classic A.D. 466-527) written by Li Daoyuan in Northern Wei Dynasty, that Tan Shuyu Temple was praised as the prominent scenic spot of the State of Jin. The temple, which experienced constant renovations and expansions in successive dynasties after Northern Wei Dynasty, has become a major complex of architecture. The whole scenic area scattering with rows upon rows of ancient buildings as well as a vast display of historical relics, is divided into southern, northern and middle parts.

At the middle part of the scenic area, the Hall of Holy Mother which was originally built in the eleventh century of Northern Song Dynasty is the main part. The Hall of Holy Mother, a grand and majestic wooden structure with beams resting on other beams spanning between the inner and outer row of columns creating a spacious portico in front, is said to be the ancestral temple for Yi Jiang, daughter of Jiang Taigong and mother of Tang Shuyu. In the shrine seated in the middle of the hall is the sculpture of Yi Jiang in rich dress. There are also 44 young maid sculptural masterpieces, each with individual expression and posture. The Hall of Holy Mother, Immortal Spring and Ancient Crouching-dragon Cypress of Zhou Dynasty ar ranked as the ''three best things'' of Jin Ancestral Temple. The cross bridge over a square fish pond in front of the hall is the famous Yuzhao Feiliang (Flying Bridge over the Fish Pond Spring). This is a cross bridge of unique design protruding both at east and west sides, just like two wings of a flying bird soaring to great height from the water surface. According to the historical record, this is the only such bridge preserved in China today.

To the east of the Flying Bridge over the Fish Pond Spring lies the Sacrifice Hall where it consecrates the oblations for the holy mother. This hall is uniquely and elegantly built, of simple layout but spacious. Viewing it from the distance, it looks like an exquisite pavilion. Jinren Platform (Iron Figure Platform) stands to the east of the Sacrifice Hall. On each corner of this platform is arrayed with an iron deity figure in two metres high. The figures appearing powerful with dignified bearing, are still shining, free of rust, demonstrating fine ancient metallurgical technology.

The old and ageless trees and the meandering limpid streams create another picturesque landscape of the temple. The poetry and calligraphy beautifully and profoundly eulogizing the temple written by Li Bai, Fan Zhongyan and Ouyang Xiu the well-known poets, add lingering charm and gracefulness to this scenery. Hence, it is noted as a dazzling pearl in the beautiful land of China.

Jin Ancestral Temple in Splendid China is reproduced on the scale of 1:15. The shape of the construction is completely true to life and the overall arrangements of the pavilions and balconies with red walls and green tiles are so ingeniously laid out that they reveal much of the ancient and quaint styles of Song architecture.

The Mausoleum of Genghis Khan

The Mausoleum of Genghis Khan is located 15 kilometres southeast of Echinehoro in Inner Mongolia.

Genghis Khan, whose name was called Temudjin, established Yuan Dynasty. During his reign, his military accomplishments were unparalled at the moment and his domain extended to Mid-Asia and South Russia. He died of an illness in 1227. According to folklore, Genghis Khan, leading his troops and passing Echinehoro, was fascinated by the beautiful scenery there and said "This shall be my burial place when I die".

The existing mausoleum, rebuilt after the liberation of China, occupies an area of over 1,500 square metres.

The main group of buildings are composed of three Mongolian-yurt-styled grand palaces communicating to the veranda buildings. The octagonal Memorial Hall in the main hall where the statue of Genghis Khan is housed is 26.6 metres high and the two corridors are covered with exquisitely painted frescoes depicting the life story of Genghis Khan. At the back hall where it once served as the bedroom are placed with four yellow Mongolian yurts to enshrine the coffins of the couple of Genghis Khan and the couple of his grandson, Gui You.

The palaces on two sides of the main hall measure 23.3 metres high. The right palace is placed with the coffins of the couple of Genghis Khan's fourth son, Tuo Lei whereas valuable relics of a long spear, a double-edged sword, saddle and tablewares once used by Genghis Khan are displayed on the left palace.

Genghis Khan died in 1227 but his coffin was moved time and again and later was put at the Taer Lamasery in Huangzhong county, Qinghai. In 1954, the state allotted money to build a new mausoleum which was completed in 1956 and the coffin was once again transported back from Qinghai to be laid in the new mausoleum on 17th March (Lunar Calendar). Thus, this date becomes the Memorial Day of Genghis Khan. Henceforth, Mongolian people from far and near gather together on the pasture of the new mausoleum to hold the memorial services and organize various kinds of traditional activities there annually.

The Mausoleum of Genghis Khan on Splendid China is reproduced on the scale of 1:15. It is constructed in an artistic, unique style. There are designs of clouds on the rooftop made by patterning together blue glazed tiles inlaid with golden yellow glazed bricks, resplendent and magnificent. Seen against white clouds drifting in a blue sky and under the shade of green trees, it looks imposing and radiant.

The Tomb of Wang Zhaojun

The story of "Wang Zhaojun, a beautiful imperial concubine went beyond the Desert to get married to the king of Xiongnu and thus contributed to the harmony between the Han Dynasty and Xiongnu" has circulated among the people in China since ancient times.. The folk artists, poets and story-tellers have created numerous fantastic, tortuous legends and poems, moving stories and plays. Many of them are in praise of Wang Zhaojun's "Heqin * Deed". Bai Juyi (772-846), the famous poet of Tang Dynasty once wrote two quatrains depicting the moving scene at the time when Wang Zhaojun, in the mood of depression, started for Xiongnu. Once the envoy of Han came to see her, she wanted him to ask Han Emperor when to buy back her freedom and not to tell him her poor condition there. Wang Zhaojun is generally recognized as one of the four beauties in ancient China (The four beauties are Wang Zhaojun, Xi Shi, Diao Chan and Yang Guifei).

Many beautiful legends express people's deep feeling of boundless love for Wang Zhaojun. A beautiful, small and weak woman, being deeply conscious of the right-eousness, voluntarily and consciously left the bustling capital city for the bitter, cold desert far away in the north and got married to Shanyu, the king of Xiongnu. The war between Han Dynasty and Xiongnu which lasted for as long as a hundred years thus turned hostility into friendship. From then on, the peoples of Han and Xiongnu

lived in peace and harmony. We deeply esteem her for her sacrifice to the benefit of the people and nation.

Wang Zhaojun, a country girl, was born in Zigui county in Hubei province. In the years of Emperor Yuan's reign in Han Dynasty, she was chosen as a concubine into the imperial palace. In 33 B.C., Emperor Yuan of Han Dynasty agreed with the demand of "Heqin" put forward by Hu Han Shanyu of Xiongnu and married Wang Zhaojun to him, and she was granted a title of "the Queen of Ning Hu", meaning "Lucky Queen" in Han language. She kept in memory her aim throughout her life in Xiongnu and made a valuable contribution to the unity and friendship of both peoples. After she died, she was buried at the south bank of the Great Black River in the suburbs of Hohhot, called Wang Zhaojun Tomb. It is said that the grass around the tomb is green in four seasons. As the ancient poem eulogizes: "No tomb has the green grass all the year round, besides Wang Zhaojun's", so it is also known as "Evergreen Tomb".

Wang Zhaojun Tomb is 33 metres high, the base of the tomb occupies an area of 1,900 square metres. It is similar in form or appearance to the ones of Qinshihuang, Hanwudi and Tangtaizong. After the founding of New China, it was renovated and maintained for many times. The verdant and luxuriant pines and cypresses, the carpet of green grass, make the scenery more enchanting. It is named "Emerald Green Tomb" and rated as one of the

eight beautiful scenes of Hohhot city.

Wang Zhaojun Tomb in Splendid China is reproduced on the scale of 1:15. In front of the tomb, there is a platform linking with the stairs. It bears some resemblances to the tomb of Hanwudi. There are two pavilions, one stands in front and the other at the top of Wang Zhaojun Tomb. With jade green grass around the tomb and full of charming multi-coloured flowers everywhere, you will feel fresh, completely relaxed and pleasant.

* "Heqin" means "to attempt to cement relations with rulers of minority nationalities in the border areas by marrying daughters of the Han imperial family to them in some feudal dynasties".

Terra Cotta Warriors and Horses of Qin Shihuang Mausoleum

Qin Shihuang Mausoleum, is 30 kilometres east of Xi'an city, south of Li Mountain and north of Wei River.

In the spring of 1974, at 1,500 metres east of Qin Shihuang Mausoleum, three huge vaults with plenty of terra cotta warriors and horses were discovered. Their magnificence and grand sight are really a great wonder in the world. The largest one is called Vault No. 1, covering an area of more than 14,000 square metres, from which the terra cotta warriors and horses unearthed are around six thousand. The figures all face the east and form into a rectangular battle array, symbolizing that they are the patrol soldiers defending the imperial mausoleum. Apart from the main 38 columns of main force, there are vanguards and flank guards. The battle formation is the same as Qin Shihuang's actual conquering army. Though they are terra cotta warriors and horses, they look grandiose, animated and lifelike as if the grand spectacle of Emperor Qin Shihuang's mighty army reappeared before your eyes.

The soldiers range from 1.8 to 1.86 metres in height, with higher ranking officers being the tallest and ordinary foot-soldiers the shortest. The arm of services can be divided into infantry, cavalry and soldiers on chariots. Judging from their appearances, the soldiers come from Guanzhong at Wei River Valley as well as from Sichuan and national minorities from the Northwest. Postures vary depending on each figure's military function: there are archers with crossbows, spearmen and swordsmen grasping their weapons, and charioteers holding bronze reins to the team of horses pulling the chariots. The warriors' uniforms and hairstyles show realistic details, and faces reveal astonishingly lifelike individual human expressions. Even the painted terra cotta horses are almost lifesize and vivid in naturalistic detail, exhibiting a spirited readiness for battle.

The terra cotta horses, each 2 metres long and 1.7 metres high, with head throwing back and mouth open, four legs standing upright and eyes piercing bright, are horses of fine breed from Hequ in Kansu province.

All the weapons, full of variety and in large number, are all real knives and swords used at that time. Among them, there is a sword made of bronze, buried in the earth for more than 2,000 years, yet it is still neither rust nor rot, glittering coldly, which proves that the technique of metallurgy is superb then.

The terra cotta warriors and horses of Qin Shihuang Mausoleum, a vast-scale, ancient military museum, has a precious, historical as well as artistic value. It is also regarded as a gem of the treasure-house of the world culture and the world's eighth wonder as well.

The Terra Cotta Warriors and Horses of Qin Shihuang Mausoleum in Splendid China is reproduced on the scale of 1:10. The solemn appearance and facial expression of the figures are true to life and there are also innumerable variation of forms. The one, "settling" in Shenzhen now, can mix the spurious with the genuine.

Big Wild Goose Pagoda

ocated in the south of ancient city, Xi'an, Big Wild Goose Pagoda was suggested to be built by the famous Tang monk, Master Xuan Zang (A.D. 602-664) for preserving a large number of Buddhist scriptures which he had collected, translated and researched in India. The construction began in A.D. 652 (the third year of Yong Hui, during the reign of Emperor Gaozhong, Tang Dynasty). Master Xuan Zang himself took part in the labour at the construction site so the project was completed smoothly.

The original pagoda, constructed according to the one in Mojietuo State in India, is a five-storey, square brick building of Indian style. The pagoda was built within the premises of Ci En Temple, thus also called Ci En Pagoda. It was restored and renovated for many times during the past 1,000 years. The present structure is a seven-storey brick pagoda of Chinese-pavilion style, a square pyramid of green brick, 64 metres high, magnificent and solid. The lintels and the frames of the gates on the bottom tier are engraved with elegant paintings of Tang style. What is more, two steles are set into the walls on either side of the south gate of the pagoda. On one stele is inscribed the "Preface to the Sacred Religion" by Tang Emperor Taizong (Li Shimin, reigned during 626-649). On the other stele is the "Chronicle of the Preface" by Emperor Taizong's son, Emperor Gaozong (Li Zhi), inscribed by the famous calligrapher Chu Suiliang of Tang Dynasty. The famous paintings and ancient books have added great charm to the place. Tu Fu, the famous Tang poet, wrote a poem in praise of the magnificence and grandeur of the pagoda.

Big Wild Goose Pagoda is succinct in shape with harmonious proportion, remarkable, solemn and in elegant taste. There are spiral stone stairs leading to the top from the bottom tier in the pagoda. If you climb up the top of it, the full view of the ancient city, Xi'an will appear before your eyes.

Big Wild Goose Pagoda in Splendid China is reproduced on the scale of 1:15. The pagoda is beautifully shaped, solid in construction, particular in design, made of green bricks with red flowers planted around it. All these make the scene more attractive.

Huangdi Tomb

 Huangdi[1] Tomb is located on the Jiaoshan Mountain to the north of Huangling county, Shaanxi province. It is also called "Jiaoling", meaning the tomb on Jiaoshan Mountain. The temple of the tomb was renovated and rebuilt many times during the dynasties of Han, Tang, Song, Ming and Qing. The present tomb, 36 metres high and 48 metres in circumference, is surrounded by the wall in 1 metre-odd high. In front of the tomb, there is an ancient tablet in the pavilion. On it the words "Jiao Ling Long Yu" were engraved, meaning "Riding a dragon at the Tomb of Jiaoshan Mountain". The legend goes that it is the place where Huangdi flew to the sky by riding a dragon. There are thousands of ancient cypresses in the temple area, the one in "Xuan Yuan Temple" at the foot of the mountain is 20 metres high, the largest one among them. It is said this cypress was planted by Huangdi, or Xuan Yuan (his first name). It is the largest ancient cypress in China, and the foreign friends eulogize it as "The Father of the Cypress" in the world.

According to the record in ancient book, Huangdi's surname is Gong Sun, his first name, Xuan Yuan and was born in Qufu, Shandong. At the age of 118, one day when he was on an inspection tour in Henan, suddenly a yellow dragon flew down and fetched him to heavenly palace.

Riding the yellow dragon, he first went to Huangling county in Shaanxi to bid farewell to his officials and people. The fellow-villagers dragged his clothes and tried to persuade him to stay but in vain. He left with them only a piece of cloth torn up from the corner of his clothes. People buried it and built up a tomb on picturesque Jiaoshan Mountain and called it Huangdi Tomb. There are thousands of green cypresses at the tomb area, proudly erect and luxuriantly green.

The tomb area, around 4,000 square metres, is surrounded with green hills and clear waters, like the Eight Diagrams[2], full of grandeur. The main building is the Great Hall of the tomb with upturned eaves, carved beams and painted pillars, resplendent and magnificent showing an atmosphere of solemnity. In the Great Hall is a stone relief of Huangdi in calm expression.

The Huangdi Tomb in Splendid China is reproduced on the scale of 1:15. The tomb is imbued with an atmosphere of grandeur and solemnity, true to life in modelling and surrounded with luxuriant, green cypresses.

1. Huangdi is regarded as the earliest ancestor of the Chinese nation.
2. The Eight Diagrams (eight combinations of three whole or broken lines formerly used in divination)

Dunhuang Magao Grottoes

agao Grottoes, also known as Thousand Buddha Caves, which are located 25 kilometres to the southeast of the east broken cliff of Mingshan Mountain in Dunhuang county of Gansu province, are the world-famous ancient art treasure of China. They started to be built at the second year of the Jian Yuan's reign in the former Qin Dynasty (A.D. 366). With repeated constructions and renovations in Sui, Tang, Song and Yuan Dynasties, there are now 492 grottoes with frescoes stretching for more than 45,000 square metres, and over 2,400 painted statues, the highest ones measuring a dozen metres and the figurines only one-tenth metre high. Some are simple and vigorous and some are small and exquisite with forms lively and vividly shaped. Buddhist history, Buddhist scripture and stories of Buddhism are drawn on the frescoes and pronounced Buddhist flavour is found in them. As seen in the frescoes, Buddhist statues are solemn, Bodhisattvas composed, Heavenly Kings mighty, the lads simple and unaffected, buildings and pavilions exquisite, rosy clouds changeable, flying Apsarases circling in the air with immortals playing music around the lotus flowers. It looks like a scene in the Pure Land.

The painted figure statues and frescoes in Magao Grottoes bear a different artistic styles due to varied social practices and eras. For instance, you will find the drawings in Northern Wei Dynasty are straightforward, uninhibited and of primitive simplicity whereas high skill and smoothness with multicolors are added into the drawings in Sui Dynasty. Furthermore, the art works in Tang Dynasty depict majesty and solemnity but not lacking gorgeousness and splendour. In a word, they all like a hundred flowers in bloom, colourful and extraordinarily splendid.

Magao Grottoes also serve as the important cultural relics for the study of China's ancient history. They are not only highly thought of at home but they also receive a great concern by the archaeologists and historians in other countries of the world forming the famous "Dunhuang Theory" Hence, Magao Grottoes are deserved to be called the sparkling pearl in China's national art treasure.

The Id Kah Mosque

Located at the northwest corner of Aidier Square of Kashgar city in Xinjiang, the Id Kah Mosque started to be built in the third year of the reign of Jia Qing in Qing Dynasty (A.D. 1798). After renovation and expansion in the 18th year of Dao Guang's reign (A.D. 1838), the mosque became the present shape. It is the largest mosque in Xinjiang.

The structure of the mosque is in the style of quadrangle. With an area of 16,800 square metres, the rectangle building consists of the arched gateway, room for lecturing the Islamic scriptures, religious service hall, pool and so on. In the Great Hall are 140 green pillars carved with patterns of flowers, arrayed in network shape and of a great momentum. At both sides of the hall are places for imam to study and engage in advanced studies. The mosque can hold seven thousand Muslims to do religious activities at one time.

Whenever Friday, the day for the Muslims to go to mosque, has come, they conscientiously come to do religious service. The most grand day is the Corban which is held once a year. Putting aside the work on hand and closing all the shops, three days in succession, the worshippers gather before the great square of the mosque and hold religious service early on the day before the morning sun rises. It is a grand spectacle.

The Id Kah Mosque in Splendid China is reproduced on the scale of 1:15. At both sides of the mosque gate stand two cylinder calling towers, unique in style as well as magnificent and majestic in appearance.

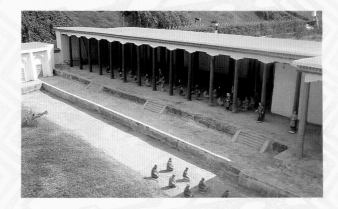

Xiang Fei's Tomb

Xiang Fei's Tomb, a family mausoleum of Xiang Fei which is also called Abakh Hoja Tomb, is located at the outskirt to the eastern gate of Kashi. The tomb was first built here for Xiang Fei in 1640 after her death. It was only a tomb containing Xiang Fei's personal effects without the remains. Xiang Fei was once illustrious at that time and hence the name Xiang Fei's Tomb.

Xiang Fei named Abakh Hoja was originally the wife of Huo Ji Zhan, a Moslem tribal chief in southern Xinjiang. In the 22nd year of Qianlong's reign (A.D. 1757) in Qing Dynasty, Emperor Qianlong, hearing that Abakh Hoja was born with a strange bodily fragrance, made her an imperial concubine and granted her the title of Xiang Fei (Fragrant Imperial Concubine). In order to relieve Xiang Fei from being homesick and to win her favour, Qianlong spent a large fortune and manpower to build a palace and high buildings in Uygur style. Among them, Baoyue Building where Xiang Fei lived, was painted on its wall with landscape paintings in style and features of Xinjiang. In addition, a huge bronze mirror measuring over 3 metres high and 1 metre wide was installed for her use of dressing and making up. Seething with national hatred, Xiang Fei finally died of depression. Before her death, she left word that she wished her remains to be sent back to her homeland. It revealed that Qianlong actually buried her in Yu Fei Mausoleum in Beijing but an empty tomb containing only Xiang Fei's personal effects was carried back to her homeland to be buried in her family mausoleum. This is where the existing Xiang Fei's Tomb or called "hao han" or "ai zi ya di" by Uygur in the locality.

Xiang Fei's Tomb is so far the largest Moslem mausoleum in China. The towering white poplars and blossoming flowers are found everywhere in the mausoleum. Standing in the centre of the mausoleum is the main hall with an area of 700 square metres and over 20 metres high. Rectangular in shape with an arched roof, the walls of the main hall are inlaid with yellow, green and blue coloured glaze. Situated at four corners are the cylindrical pagodas. The whole hall, dazzling with brightness and radiance and displaying surpassing beauty and magnificence, is characterized with the distinctive national style and Moslem flavour. Fifty-eight Moslem dome-shaped tombs are preserved in the hall whereas Xiang Fei's Tomb is located at the left rear corner of the hall. The frontage of the tomb are engraved with three Chinese characters " 香妃墓 ", meaning "Xiang Fei's Tomb", thus adding to this ancient mausoleum a boundless legendary and romantic colour.

Xiang Fei's Tomb in Splendid China is reproduced on the scale of 1:15. Its shape is constructed in architectural pattern exhibiting an elegant outlook. A strong Moslem style is fully displayed by the selection of the yellow, green and blue coloured glaze inlaid on the exterior walls.

Potala Palace

Standing on the Red Mount of Lhasa in Tibet is Potala Palace which rises to the summit. The Palace, measuring 118 metres high and covering an area of 130,000 square metres, almost takes up the whole of the Red Mount. It is the most magnificent, solemn and sacred place in the hearts of the Buddhists.

White Palace, the main building of Potala Palace, with the white outside wall, serves both as the residence and halls holding religious activities of the Dalai Lamas in successive generations. The upper part of the White Palace, where the living room of the Dalai Lamas is located, includes the Pilgrimage Hall, Buddhist Scripture Study Hall, Law-Protection Hall and the bedroom of Dalai, etc. The design of this building is so exquisite with sunshine illuminating all the year round hence it gets the name of "Sunlight Hall". This Hall is luxuriously decorated in which there is a full display of jewellery, Buddhist figures and musical instruments used in the Buddhist mass.

Red Palace, with the red outside wall, lies in the west of the White Palace. This is a multi-storey building consisting of the main hall, the Buddhist Hall and the Tomb Pagoda Hall of the Dalai Lamas. It is the major architectural complex of Potala Palace. With the most artistic characteristics, Tomb Pagoda Hall is used for keeping the bodies of Dalai Lamas of generations. The bodies are preserved in ashes and put in the tomb pagoda to be worshipped by the disciples. These pagodas are all heavily coloured and gold-plated inlaid with precious jewels and jade. The fifth tomb is the most extravagant and it stands as high as 16 metres with an area of 452 square metres. 11,900 taels of gold were used in its gold plating inlaid with innumerable precious jewellery and over 4,000 pearls were used. It can be rated as the priceless treasure in the world.

Inside Potala Palace, you may be amazed by the colourful sculptures and paintings and thus it deserves the title of art gallery and museum.

Potala Palace was initially built at the time of A.D. 641 when Tubo King Srongtsan Gampo was married to Princess Wen Cheng but after numerous constructions and expansions, it made itself a good example of the ancient Tibetan culture and architecture. It is thus reputed as "A pearl on the roof of the world".

For resembling the real object, Potala Palace in Splendid China is constructed in a way to show that its appearance looks like a powerful lion in prone position with summits towering in the sky displaying grandeur and magnificence. The palace is reproduced on the scale of 1:15. In order to protrude the golden roof top of the main building, 15,000 pieces of goldleaf are used. There are grand palaces within palaces. The palace stands so high that it resembles a magnificent castle in the heaven. All this concentrates to symbolize the fine tradition and unique characteristics of the ancient Tibetan architecture.

I n the south of Chongxing Temple in Beizhen county town of Liaoning province stand twin Buddhist pagodas existent in China, called "Twin Pagodas in Chongxing Temple".

Started to be built in Liao Dynasty, the twin pagodas were restored and renovated for many times in Yuan, Ming, Qing Dynasties and they are preserved well until now. The twin pagodas stand east and west in the opposite direction with a distance of 43 metres. Octagon and multi-eaves in shape, the twin pagodas are made of brick in thirteen storeys. On the top of each pagoda, there are carved-brick circular arches, balustrades with words on its, lotus flowers, etc. At each corner, a carved warrior is seen in the manner of bearing heavy load. At the centre of each face of the pagoda, there is an arched niche, a sitting Buddha is carved in the middle of it. An attendant stands on each side of it. Above it, there are Buddha's canopies, apsaras, etc. The lower layers under the eaves are carved-brick circular arches. The upper-layers with brick upturned eaves diminish inwardly at each tier. On the top of the pagodas are found lotus thrones, nectar vessels, pearls, etc.

The Twin Pagodas in Chongxing Temple in Splendid China is reproduced on the scale of 1:15. The construction of the pagodas follows out the original and preserves the style and features of the real object.

Twin Pagodas in Chongxing Temple

The City God Temple

he City God Temple is located at Yu Yuan Bazaar in Shanghai city. According to legend, it was originally built by the King of Wu, Sun Hao in the Three Kingdoms Period (220-265), then rebuilt in Ming Dynasty and reconstructed again in 1926. Now it has become a favourite place for sight-seeing in Shanghai.

Recently the main hall of the City God Temple was renovated. The reliefs of Huang Zhong and Guan Yunchang, the famous generals in the Three Kingdoms Period, were separately carved meticulously on the right and left sides of the hall. At both ends of the ridge are upturned eaves with dragons mounting the clouds. In the middle of the ridge are a set of lifelike reliefs regarding "To be Sworn Brothers between Liu Pei, Guan Yu and Zhang Fei in the Peach Garden" narrated in the Romance of the Three Kingdoms. Embellished with more than a hundred of palace lanterns vying with each other, the main hall looks colourful and resplendent. At the Good Fortune Room in the main hall, there are a colourful drawing of dragon and phoenix (showing good luck), figure paintings of the Three Kingdoms covering all over the glass in the windows, antique padauk tea set and chairs. The pavilion is indeed a splendid sight. At the back of the main hall, there is a Maiden Hall with the Statue of Bodhisattva to be solemnly and respectfully worshipped by people. Setting off by the calligraphists carved on the lintels over the doors by famous calligraphists, the whole hall looks pretty and elegant.

The City God Temple in Splendid China is reproduced on the scale of 1:15. The temple built of white walls, grey tiles and crimson windows, together with the Zigzag Bridge over the shining, silvery ripples, fully shows the beauty of water village in southern China.

Memorial Temple of Zhuge Liang

Zhuge Liang[1] is a respected historical figure known even to women and children. At the end of Western Jin Dynasty, Li Xiong, the king of Zhen (Han) Kingdom in the Sixteen States Periods, built a temple in memory of Zhuge Liang, the Prime Minister of the Kingdom of Shu in the Three Kingdoms Period, and it was called Wuhou Temple or the Temple of Marquis Wu. The original Wuhou Temple built by Li Xiong was located in Shaocheng of Chengdu city, then it was moved at the side of Liu Bei[2] Temple in the southern suburbs of the city. At the beginning of Ming Dynasty (A.D. 1368), the two temples were merged into one. In the 11th year of the reign of Kang Xi in Qing Dynasty (A.D. 1672), when it was rebuilt, an additional Hall of Zhuge Liang was set up.

At the centre of the Hall is seated Zhuge Liang Statue. On its left are the statues of his son, Zhuge Zhan and grandson, Zhuge Shang. Inside and outside the hall, there are a number of couplets and plaques, among them the most famous one is the antithetical couplet written by Zhao Fan in Qing Dynasty, which means "If you know how to make a psychological attack, you will persuade an offender to confess. When you make a policy or decision, you must think it over according to historical conditions and objective reality". At the side of Zhuge Liang Statue, there is a stone tablet of Prime Minister of Shu, Zhuge Wuhou in the temple with a record of events inscribed on it. It was erected in the 4th year of Yuan Hou's reign in Tang Dynasty (A.D. 809).

The stone tablet was composed by the then famous Prime Minister Fei Du, written by the calligrapher Liu Gongzhou and engraved by the sculptor Lu Jian. The excellent essay, calligraphy and carving all made by famous experts, are acclaimed as the "Three-Best Tablet" as well as a "gem" of Wuhou Temple.

Du Fu, the great poet of Tang Dynasty wrote the following lines in praise of Zhuge Liang:

"Where to find the deceased Prime Minister's temple?
Outside Chengdu, under the cypress arch ample.
The grass round the steps reflects the colour of spring;
The oriole amid the leaves vainly sings it strain.
Thrice the Emperor to him came for the plan to rule;
Two reigns[3] the noble statesman served heart and soul.
Before seeing victory, he died in the camp ground,
It oft makes later heroes weep with sighs profound!"

From this poem, we can deeply feel what rare gifts and

bold strategy and historical feats he has possessed.

The Memorial Temple of Zhuge Liang in Splendid China is reproduced on the scale of 1:15. Zhuge Liang is seated at the temple in serene posture with his son, Zhuge Zhan and grandson, Zhuge Shang on both sides, vivid and lifelike.

1. Zhuge Liang (A.D. 181-234), the Prime Minister of the Kingdom of Shu, the famous statesman and strategist in the period of the Three Kingdoms (220-265).
2. Liu Bei, emperor of the Kingdom of Shu.
3. Zhuge Liang had served Emperor Liu Bei (161-230) and his son Liu Chan (207-271).

Leshan Grand Buddha Statue

Leshan Grand Buddha Statue is located on Mt. Lingyun in Leshan of Sichuan, at the confluence of the Minjiang, Dadu and Qingyi Rivers. The Buddha Statue is carved out on the cliff overlooking the rivers. As the legend goes, Monk Haitong in Tang Dynasty, seeing that boats often got capsized in the turbulent water, started the construction of the Buddha Statue to suppress the evil spirit. The Buddha Statue, in a sitting position, was hewn out on the cliff of Mt. Lingyun, hence it also got the name of "Lingyun Grand Buddha Statue". According to the record of "Grand Buddha Statue of Lingyun Temple in Jiazhou", the construction of the grand Buddha took 91 years altogether. It started to be built by the famous Monk Haitong in the year of Kai Yuan in Tang Dynasty (A.D. 713) and completed by Governor Wei Gao of Tian Nan, Sichuan in the 19th year of Zhen Yuan (A.D. 803). The head of the Buddha is above the mountain with feet resting on the river. It is 71 metres tall, its shoulders 28 metres wide and its nose 5.6 metres long. Its instep is large enough to accommodate more than one hundred people and it is so far such the largest stone carving in the world. On the right side of the Buddha is the zigzag plank road of Lingyun Cliff advancing tortuously downward to reach the river. People used to say: "The mountain itself is the statue and the statue is the mountain". "The Buddha wears a solemn posture and dignified expression. Its feet stamp on the ground to form a majestic and powerful spirit. The appearance of its resting on a lotus throne against the background of mountain and rivers gives an outlook that it seems to come from the sky or to emerge from the ground". Its form is superbly shaped thus winning a high praise and admiration from all.

Leshan Grand Buddha Statue in Splendid China is reproduced on the scale of 1:8. Its solemn appearance is outlined in a bold hand but of rich content and succinct style with harmonious proportion. It wears a composed and calm expression exhibiting elegance and unconventional gracefulness of its own.

Dazu Stone Carvings

azu Stone Carvings are located at Dazu county which is abundant with stone sculptures, Buddhist statues and inscriptions on tablets. They were first built in late Tang Dynasty and popular in two Song Dynasties. They are such an agglomeration of artistic stone inscriptions and also the precious remains on Buddhism of artistic stone carvings in China for over 1,000 years. The sculptures are distributed in over 40 places with more than 50,000 Buddhist statues but they are mostly found in Beishan Hill and Baoding Hill in such a large scale and exquisite in skill which is rarely seen in China. Hence they rank among the first batch of the important cultural relics under the state protection. People used to say that the Baoding Hill stone carvings in this scenic site started its construction by an eminent Buddhist monk, Zhao Zhifeng in Song Dynasty and took over 70 years to complete the whole project. It has 13 places housing over 10,000 Buddhist statues. Among them, the Big and Miniature Buddha Bend, 1,000-hand Bodhisattva inside the niche, Yuanjue Cave in a variety of forms are the most famous and Big Buddha Bend is the cream of all. These stone carvings are divided into 19 series of representations like a consistent picture-story book in ancient times which are exquisitely designed and ingeniously arranged. The Bodhisattva inside the niche extends her 1,030 hands like a peacock spreading its tails. Her hands stretch out in upward, left and right directions with hands holding various kinds of musical instruments in multifarious patterns, none identical to each other. All this composes a magnificent scene. There is also a 31-metre-long reclining Buddha with only the upper part of the body engraved.

Dazu Stone Carvings in Splendid China are reproduced on the scale of 1:5. They are large scale in form. Its stone statues are beautifully shaped and really true to life and its expression natural and charming, completely displaying majesty and splendour.

Shengshou Monastery

ocated on Baoding Mountain, 15 kilometres northeast of Da Zu county town, Sichuan province, Shengshou Monastery started to be built in Song Dynasty (A.D. 960-1279). Later it lay waste. The present Shengshou Monastery was built in Ming and Qing Dynasties. The main buildings are the Devaraja (Heavenly King) Hall, Jade Emperor Hall, Buddha Hall, Buddhist Scriptures Hall, Light-Oil-Lamp Hall, Wei Mo Hall (the highest one which is built at the foot of the mountain), in which a stone-carved statue of Wei Mo Reclining Buddha is found.

The Shengshou Monastery in Splendid China is reproduced in accordance with the one in Sichuan on the scale of 1:15. Apart from the distribution of the halls, the unique characteristics of the corner towers are still preserved.

Du Fu's Thatched Cottage

 u Fu, the great poet of Tang Dynasty, was born in 712 and died in 770. He experienced the most prosperous period of the era of Kai Yuan, Tang Dynasty as well as the terrible hard days of "Anshi Riot". The splendid poems, embodied his sympathy for the people living in great misery, are widely read generation after generation.

"In the Eight Moon, the autumn gales howl from on high, The thrice-laid thatch rolls from my roof to the sky."

"If there were spacious houses, thousands and more, Sheltering all the world to the joy of the poor."

"Alas! I'd prefer my cot ruins, I myself frozen to death." These are the lines from his famous poem, "Ode to My Cottage Unroofed by the Autumn Gales". It is said that the poem was written after his cottage built between 759-765, on the side of the Huanhua (Flower-Bathing) Brook in the western suburbs of Chengdu was destroyed by the autumn gales. To commemorate the great poet, the officials and civilians of Chengdu city renovated the thatched cottage of Du Fu in the late years of Tang Dynasty (907). It was rebuilt twice in Ming and Qing Dynasties. Occupying an area of 20 hectares, the cottage is set in a scene of calm and beauty, embellished with small bridges, a meandering brook, dark green bamboos and tall ancient trees.

Du Fu's Thatched Cottage in Splendid China is reproduced on the scale of 1:15, resembling the real object.

Dr. Sun Yat-sen's Mausoleum

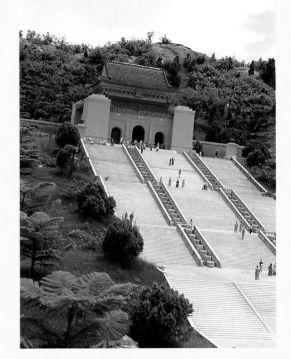

Located at the southern foot of Maoshan in the middle part of Purple Mountain, the Mausoleum of China's great revolutionary forerunner, Dr. Sun Yat-sen stands erect with the majestic green hills behind it, with Xiaoling (the tomb of Zhu Yuanzhang, the founding emperor of Ming Dynasty) to the east, and the famous Ling Gu Temple to the west.

The construction of the mausoleum began in January 1926 but the main structure was completed in June 1, 1929, and the burial ceremony was held as well. In 1933, the whole construction was finished. The mausoleum, facing south, built at the foot of the mountain, covers an area of more than 45,000 mu and its ground plan is in the shape of a huge bell, with which, so to speak, symbolizing the lofty ideal of struggling in Mr. Sun's whole life.

At the entrance of the mausoleum, there is a huge stone gateway, on the lintel engraved with six Chinese characters "自由、平等、博愛", meaning, "Freedom, Equality and Brotherhood".

The entrance of the gateway is located at the central line of the tomb avenue, 375 metres long and 40 metres wide, leading directly to the spacious square in front of the mausoleum.

Passing through the square, you will come to the front

gate of the mausoleum. The transom over the gate is inscribed with four Chinese characters "天下爲公" (The country belongs to all people) in Dr. Sun Yat-sen's own handwriting. The Burial Chamber solemnly stands halfway up the mountain at the height of 158 metres. From the front gate to this chamber, there are 399 stone steps in all. When you look up on the ground, the chamber is imposingly magnificent and full of grandeur.

After climbing the steps, you will find a terrace with an area of 6,156 square metres. To the north of it are the magnificent and solemn Memorial Hall and Burial Chamber. This is a palace-styled building, with double upturned eaves, covered under a traditional-styled roof of blue-glazed tile, measuring 28 metres long, 22 metres deep, and 26 metres high. At the centre of the Memorial Hall, there is a stone seated statue of Mr. Sun. Around the stone pedestal, there are many pieces of relief sculptures relating to the stories of the revolutionary activities of Mr. Sun. At the middle of the north wall, there is a door leading to the Burial Chamber. A stone coffin is placed in the centre of the Memorial Hall, the clean, white granite statue of Mr. Sun lying horizontally on it. Under the statue, the remains of Mr. Sun is buried.

The new materials, new style and the traditional palace-typed modelling are adopted in the construction of the mausoleum. It is a model of modern mausoleum architecture in which the national style is harmoniously integrated with the art of modern architecture.

Dr. Sun Yat-sen's Mausoleum in Splendid China is reproduced on the scale of 1:15. The scope of construction and the overall layout resemble the one in Nanjing.

Slender West Lake

Slender West Lake is located in the western suburbs of Yangzhou city, Jiangsu province. After repeated constructions in six successive dynasties, it has gradually become a scenic spot. Its name has derived from the shape of the lake, long, slim and winding. When compared with West Lake, its scenery is small but graceful and exquisite. A poem written by Wang Hang, a poet of Qiantang, Qing Dynasty, depicting the beauty of Slender West Lake, adds more fame to it.

The architectural art of China's ancient garden is so skillfully applied that the pavilions, buildings, waterside pavilions and winding corridors are constructed in a way to match harmoniously with the surrounding landscape. The scenic sites of the Rainbow Bridge, the Long Causeway with Spring Willows, Minor Jinshan Hill, Five-Pavilion Bridge and the White Dagoba scatter alongside the lake.

"Yangzhou is good and the Rainbow Bridge ranks the first". The Rainbow Bridge, which arches across the east and west banks of the lake like a rainbow, is praised to be the number-one scenery in Yangzhou. After crossing the Rainbow Bridge, the Long Causeway with Spring Willows, one of the 24 sceneries of Yangzhou, emerges. When the flowers blossom in the warm spring season, the fragrance of flowers and the song of the orioles which concerted with the pink peach blossom and green willow will surely make you enchanted and charmed.

Looking through the gate at the Xu Garden, originally known as Taohua Wu (Peach-Blossom Place), the peculiar stones, the trees luxuriant but well-spaced, buildings as well as pavilions setting each other off are all like the silhouettes in the mirror. The Wind Pavilion of the Minor Jinshan Hill, which is a hillock piled up by the earth excavated from the lake, is the vantage point to have a fine view of the scenery in and around the lake. The unique style of Five-Pavilion Bridge, which measures 34 metres long, has on it five interlinking and symmetrized pavilions, majestic and gorgeous. They are forming a pattern of five lotus flowers blossoming on the lake, hence it is also called the Five-Lotus Bridge.

Slender West Lake, 4 kilometres long, is rich with sceneries that one simply cannot take them all in.

Slender West Lake in Splendid China is reproduced on the scale of 1:15. The fineness in architecture of this garden renders itself an outstanding features. The densely arrayed bamboo trees and its charming scenery will certainly make you feel joyous and enchanted.

"When the moon goes down in heavy frost the crows caw,

I'm gloomily dozing off in the fisherman's cabin by a flickering light,

Here is the Hanshan Temple which stands outside the city of Suzhou,

Welcoming the approach of a sailing boat chimes the bell in the deep of night."

Hanshan Temple at Maple Bridge, Suzhou becomes world famous and is immortalized ever since this poem "Anchoring alongside the Maple Bridge at night" which has won universal praise was composed by Zhang Ji, a poet in Tang Dynasty. Hanshan Temple, also known as Fengqiao (Maple Bridge) Temple, is located at Fengqiao town, five kilometres to the west of Suzhou city. It was initially constructed during the reign of Tianjian (A.D. 502-519) in Liang Dynasty with a history of over 1,400 years. The temple was originally called "Universal Enlightenment Joss-House". An eminent monk, Han Shan from Wu Tai Shan Mountain took charge in the temple during the reign of Zhen Guan of Tang Dynasty. In commemoration of Han Shan, the temple was renamed as Hanshan Temple by the later generations.

At that time, Han Shan and Shi De, two monks from Wu Tai Shan Mountain, resided in this temple. Later, Shi De went to Japan and constructed a temple known as Shide Temple. Henceforth, Hanshan Temple and Shide Temple become renowned both in China and Japan. It is owing to the chimes of the temple bell which is said to have the power of driving away misery and worry throughout one's life that innumerable Buddhists from Japan visit Hanshan Temple in every new year's time.

Although Hanshan Temple is a small-scale temple, its main architecture — the Hall of the Great Buddha yet appears majestic and stately with a gold-glazed and painted Sakyamuni Buddha sitting up straight in the centre of the altar. There is also in the temple a Corridor of Steles containing many stone tablets engraved with essays and poems of notables such as Yue Fei, Wen Zhengming and Tang Bohu, and these form another characteristics of the temple.

Hanshan Temple in Splendid China is reproduced on the scale of 1:15. Viewing the temple from the distance, one will find out that the temple possesses a distinguished feature of an academy but is not alike the other temples.

Hanshan Temple

Fishermen's Net Garden

Fishermen's Net Garden was built in Southern Song Dynasty (A.D. 1127-1279). It is the smallest of all the gardens in Suzhou and is also the treasure of the classic garden architecture in southern China. Moreover, it was evaluated in 1985 as one of the ten great scenic areas in China. In 1981, Ming Xuan (Bright Chamber), a Chinese-style courtyard garden, was duplicated after Fishermen's Net Garden and exported to the Metropolitan Art Museum of New York, U.S.A. Fishermen's Net Garden was once the old site of Rich Collection Hall in Southern Song Dynasty or known as "Fisherman's Retreat" but later it fell into disrepair. During Qian Long's reign in Qing Dynasty (1736-1796), it was rebuilt by Song Guanglu who possibly compared himself as the fisherman. Hence the name Fishermen's Net Garden.

Fishermen's Net Garden linking up with the living quarters to form an integral part covers only a total area less than half a hectare. In spite of its small size, it is noted for its adroit arrangement and nice designing. A small-scale man-made lake with green and limpid water is located in the centre of the garden. The grotesque and precipitous rockeries with peculiar rocks form a delightful contrast with its inverted reflection in water. Crisscrossed waterways flow to the southeast and northwest of the lake, like a trickling, long stream, holding in store a natural and lingering charm. To the east of the lake is the residential suite with a main door leading to the inner chambers. The main hall Xiao Shan Cong Cui Veranda stands to the south of the lake. Clumps of rocks, winding corridors are present with the aroma of orange osmanthus wafted in the air forming a peaceful and serene environment. On its northern side, a pavilion named Zhuoying Pavilion spans over water. From there, either watching fish from the

pavilion or savouring tea is an amusing enjoyment. To the north of the mid-lake pavilion extends a vast field of vision where the exquisitely built Zhu Wai Yi Zhi Veranda emerges but Kan Song Du Hua Veranda and Jixu Study appear indistinctly right behind Songshi Corridor forming a sharp contrast to each other. All these are so naturally inborn that no trace of artificial ornateness can be found.

There is a small garden to the northwest side of the lake where bamboo shoots are sticking out marvellously and flowers in full bloom. Facing with Hanbi Spring to the southwest corner, they all look poetic and picturesque.

On three sides of the garden are scattered with elegantly and gracefully designed small gardens. Despite the limited space, these gardens are so ingeniously laid out. When you stroll along the garden, it will give you a sense that there are gardens within gardens, scenes after scenes and at each step, a beautiful sight will meet your eyes unexpectedly. Everywhere you will have the feeling of freshness, serenity, leisure and comfort.

Fishermen's Net Garden in Splendid China, which is reproduced on the scale of 1:15, is beautifully shaped. Its architecture in labyrinth-style with ripples of upturned eaves is considered as a typical and unique example of Suzhou garden.

The Yellow Crane Tower

he sage on yellow crane was gone amid clouds white.

To what avail is Yellow Crane Tower left here?
Once gone, the yellow crane will ne'er on earth alight,
Only white clouds still float in vain from year to year.''

The poem, composed by the famous poet Cui Ho in Tang Dynasty to praise the Yellow Crane Tower, adds boundless poetic flavour to this legendary tower of long-standing history.

The Yellow Crane Tower originally stood erect on the Snake Hill of Wuchang and started to be built in A.D. 223, the 2nd year of Huangwu Reign of Wu (one of the Three Kingdoms). The tower was damaged and rebuilt time and again in various dynasties, therefore "its construction and destruction on many occasions could not be recorded". The history about its name also differs. One said that an immortal Zi An flew over this place hence got the name. Or it was said Fei Wen Wei of Shu State, after becoming an immortal, rode a yellow crane and rested here. The other legend said a Taoist priest, who returned his gratitude to the lady wine proprietor, drew a yellow crane on the wall. When the drinkers clapped hands, the yellow crane flew out from the picture and danced. All these legends are connected with immortals and the Yellow Crane Tower thus becomes world-famous.

The shape of the Yellow Crane Tower is an enigma. Experienced with wear and tear for years and destroyed many times by fire, each renovation of the tower gave a new look to it, which thus differed from the original structure. The huge fire in 1911 caused the Yellow Crane Tower all gone. We can only learn from the historical records or poetry that the "building stands at three storeys, circular outside and rectangular inside", showing quite a magnificent view.

The colourful Yellow Crane Tower standing erect on the Snake Hill started to be built in 1982 and completed three years later. The five-storey pagoda structure, added with the 5-metre-long calabash-like roof top, is at a height of 51.4 metres. The tower is covered with yellow glazed tiles with upturned eaves and corners, overlapping and piling one after another. The jingling of the aeolian bells resembles the long cry of the yellow crane. The tower is spectacular for its colourful paintings and exquisite sculptures. Its appearance, solemn and of primitive simplicity, stands elegantly and gracefully. The front and rear parts of the tower are fitted with gates, memorial archways and corridors inscribed with poetry. The newly built Yellow Crane Tower not only retains its unique characteristics of ancient architecture but also looks much more gorgeous and splendid. Climbing up the tower, a bird's eye view from above will present you a panoramic view of the mighty Changjiang River, the magnificent Yangtze River Bridge and the whole scenery of Wuhan.

The Yellow Crane Tower in Splendid China is reproduced on the scale of 1:15. Viewing the tower from the distance, the balconies and corridors are hanging with colourful Chinese calligraphic works and scroll paintings. Elegance and splendour are all shown in its decoration.

Yueyang Tower

 "Either Dongting Lake or Yueyang Tower has the best scenery under heaven". Yueyang Tower, the famous ancient architecture located at Yueyang city, Hunan province, was historically used as the parade ground where General Lu Su of the State of Wu in the Three Kingdoms Period (A.D. 215) manoeuvred his navy. At the fourth year of Kai Yuan's reign in Tang Dynasty (A.D. 716), a senior officer banished to Yue prefecture, rebuilt the tower and renamed it as Yueyang Tower. The tower was extensively restored at the fifth year of Qing Li's reign (A.D. 1045) in Song Dynasty by Teng Zijing who then stationed his troops at Ba Ling prefecture. A famous writer, Fan Zhongyan composed a prose "On the Yueyang Tower" and the tower hence enjoyed a high reputation and became one of the renowned scenic spots in southern China. The existing tower was rebuilt in the sixth year of the reign of Tong Zhi (A.D. 1867) in Qing Dynasty, retaining the artistic characteristics of the architecture of Song Dynasty.

Yueyang Tower, imposingly stands besides Lake Dongting exhibiting splendour and majesty. Taking a bird's-eye view from the tower, one becomes intrigued and intoxicated by the beautiful scenery of the vast expanse of mists and ripples as well as the reflections of the sailing boats over the lake. Made entirely of wood and by the use of interlocking brackets, Yueyang Tower was constructed without using a single nail. Its form is of primitive simplicity and the tower thus gains an unprecedented recognition and is listed together with Yellow Crane Tower of Hubei province and Tangwangge Mansion of Jiangxi province as the three most well-known towers in southern China. Li Bai, Du Fu, Bai Juyi and Li Shangyin, the famous poets in Tang Dynasty visited the tower and wrote down numerous distinguished poems which were widely read with admiration by later generations.

The tower is a three-storey wooden structure in rectangular shape, measuring at the height of 19.72 metres. The exterior of the upper storey looking like the helmet of an ancient knight with the upturned eaves of the yellow glaze-tiled roof lends a striking gracefulness to the building. The tower ranks the largest helmet-like ancient architecture in China. On both sides of the tower stand the "Drunk Three Times Pavilion", "In Memory of Du Fu Pavilion" and the "Fairy Plum Pavilion" which were built in the memory of Lu Dongbin and Du Fu.

Yueyang Tower in Splendid China is reproduced on the scale of 1:15. Its image is antique and quaint and its bee-hive-like system of brackets are exquisitely and delicately inserted between the columns and crossbeams under the helmet and it retains an artistic and unique characteristics of the ancient architecture.

Dali Three Ancient Pagodas

 Dali Three Ancient Pagodas are situated in the north of Dali city. Three Pagodas tower aloft westward to the Cangshan Mountain which is famous for its fantastic and varied forms of clouds and eastward to the mirror-like Erhai Lake. Green pine trees, flowers and other plants scatter around. Green mountains and limpid water present one of the panoramic view of the western Yunnan.

The major pagoda, Qianxunta Pagoda, which was built during the Kingdom Period of Tang Dynasty (the 9th century) is a crystallization of the cultural exchange between Han nationality of Tang Dynasty and Bai nationality of Dali, Yunnan. The pagoda is constructed in the shape of multi-eaved roofs and is the only highest brick pagoda of Tang Dynasty. It is rectangular, 69.3 metres high and is divided into 16 tiers. The base measuring 1.7 metres in diameter, is engraved with four big characters, "Yong Zhen Shan Chuan", meaning "eternal suppression to the evil beings of the rivers and mountains". From the second tier above, each tier has niches on four sides. On both diagonal sides, Buddhas are enshrined and worshipped and the remaining two sides with windows letting sunshine in. Four 7-metre high golden-winged birds, made of bronze, mount on four corners of the top tier. It is said that long time ago when the tourist dropped a piece of stone on the ground, the bird would make out a sound which seemed like melody coming from the paradise. The top roof of the pagoda is composed of metal pole, round cover and calabash-shaped pinnacle. Inside the pagoda, the middle part is hollow and the lower tier measures 13 metres high. The gate opens at the west. Entering the pagoda, stairs are seen leading to the top tier. The pagoda, bold and tall, graceful and elegant, is the typical style of pagoda in Tang Dynasty.

The other two smaller pagodas, each about 42 metres high, started to be built in the 10th century by the end of Five Dynasties during the Yunnan Dali State Period. Octagonal in shape, each pagoda has 10 tiers. Together with Qianxunta Pagoda, they form like the three legs of the tripod. Viewing the pagoda from the sky, the three pagodas stand like three tall, giant pillars. Thus, they have been called the "tashijinji" sacred place since Qing

Dynasty.

The Three Ancient Pagodas originally formed part of the Ancient Chongsheng Temple, hence the name Chongsheng Three Pagodas. Chongsheng Temple was destroyed leaving only the three unique pagodas to adorn the beautiful scenery of Cangshan Mountain and Erhai Lake.

The Three Ancient Pagodas in Splendid China are reproduced on the scale of 1:15. Its peculiar shape bears a resemblance to the Small Wild Goose Pagoda of Xi'an but retains its outstanding features.

Jingzhen Octagonal Pavilion

L ocated on Jingzhen Mountain 14 kilometres in the west of Menghai county town, Yunnan province, Jingzhen Octagonal Pavilion was first built in the 40th year of Kang Xi's reign in Qing Dynasty (A.D. 1701 or 1063 the Dai calendar). The pavilion was built in memory of Sakyamuni, the founder of Buddhism. It got the shape by imitating Sakyamuni's golden hat, and the eight angles on pavilion represented his eight senior diciples. The pavilion consists of three parts: base, body and top. The base is built of 亞 -shaped bricks in refraction angles. The body is constructed in polygon brick walls, with four doors opened on it. Both sides of the wall are painted with orange mud, inlaid with stained glasses and printed with the designs of various kinds of flowers and plants, animals and figure paintings, brilliant and dazzling to the eye. The top is a wooden structure, in the shape of tapered, multi-tier eaves, the surface covered with flat tiles like fish scale. The ridges of the roofs are adorned with traditional pottery flowers and birds decorations, and the bronze bells hung under the eaves. The pole of the pavilion is carved with the designs of flowers and plants as well as fitted with a piece of thin silver. There are many whistle-like small holes on the thin metal piece of the umbrella-shaped pavilion top. When the wind blows, the whistles sound. It is quite peculiar and marvellous. The pavilion, exquisite and splendid in structure, magnificent in shape, is the essence of the art of architecture of the Dai Buddhism.

The Jingzhen Octagonal Pavilion in Splendid China is reproduced on the scale of 1:15. The various carvings and colour paintings as well as the shape of the pavilion are exquisite and graceful. Viewing from afar, it seems that the small pavilions are built upon the big ones, layer after layer. It is really a creation of art in unique style.

Penglai Mansion

Atop a cliff of Danya Mountain in the north of Penglai county stands the magnificent Penglai Mansion. Started to be built during the reign of Emperor Jia You and Zhi Ping of Song Dynasty (1056-1063), the mansion was extended in Ming Dynasty and rebuilt in Qing Dynasty. It is a two-storey wooden building in ancient Chinese style, 15 metres high, with winding corridors around it. Hanging over the main hall is a horizontal board inscribed with the words "Penglai Mansion" painted in gold, which were written by Tie Bao, a noted calligrapher of Qing Dynasty.

Penglai Mansion, overlooking the sea, at a great distance above sea level, appears to be hanging in mid-air. The milky sea mist, like pieces of lace, shrouds it elegantly, so remarkably, and Penglai is described by the ancients as a fairyland. The whole complex of ancient buildings are divided into three courtyards, consisting of more than one hundred various halls, temples, pavilions and terraces in all. Inscriptions on the tablets and stone inscriptions of Song, Ming, Qing Dynasties are found everywhere. It is said that Penglai was once a fairy mountain in which fairies were living and effective medicine herbs of "living forever and never getting old" were growing. As it is recorded in history, Emperors Qin Shihuang and Emperor Wu of Han Dynasty had ever been there seeking for this kind of herb. According to

legend, Penglai was the place where "Eight Fairies embarked on their voyage across the sea". It is reported that the rare mirage once suddenly appeared here. Those who chanced upon it all marveled at this great wonder of nature. In "A Poem of Mirage" written by Su Shi, describing those images and scenes, he made Penglai all the more mystical. Penglai Mansion has long been famous for "The First Mansion under Heaven".

Penglai Mansion in Splendid China is reproduced on the scale of 1:15. With unique characteristics, the mansion is graceful and exquisite in its architectural art and design.

Manfeilong Pagoda

anfeilong Pagoda is situated at the rear part of Manfeilong Hill of Daimenglong in Jin Hong county, Yunnan province. As legend goes, this white pagoda was one of the three pagodas to be first built when Buddhism introduced into Xishuangbanna.

The pagoda is composed of nine big and small pagodas. The white pagoda with its golden pinnacles resembles a cluster of spring bamboo shoots breaking through the earth after rainfall, hence it is also called the "Bamboo-shoot Pagoda". The pagoda, made up of bricks and stones, was built in the year of 565 of the Dai Calendar (A.D. 1203) and was the Hinayana (Little Vehicle) Buddhist architecture. The pagoda forests are constructed on the circular base which measures 3.9 metres high. The major pagoda, 16.29 metres high, is located in the centre with eight small pagodas each 8.3 metres high arrayed octagonally and scattered around housing niches with Buddhist statues. Each pagoda, like a semicircular alms bowl, is built on the 3-layer Buddhist lotus throne. The top of the pagoda is composed of the wheel sign and nectar vessel on the lotus throne. On a primary rock beneath the niche in the south, there is a print of a human foot which is said to be the "footprints of Sakyamuni". It was because of this that a pagoda was erected to commemorate the event. Various kinds of sculptures and reliefs as well as coloured paintings matching harmoniously, represent the unique and traditional style of Dai nationality. It is also the famous scenic spot in the district of Dai nationality.

Manfeilong Pagoda in Splendid China is reproduced on the scale of 1:15. Its main pagoda is located in the centre with the other eight spread out around it in an octagonal shape. The whole group of pagodas, arranged like a circle with its base also in circular layers, shows the unique design of the architecture of Dai nationality.

Zhenghai Tower

henghai Tower, one of the eight sceneries in Guangzhou, imposingly stands on top of the renowned Yuexiu Hill. From the top floor of the tower, one can get a full panoramic view of Guangzhou city. It is said that the tower was built in the thirteenth year of Hong Wu's reign in Ming Dynasty (A.D. 1380) by Zhu Liangzhou, Prince Yong Jia who at that time garrisoned in Guangdong. The name of "Zhenghai Tower" takes the meaning of "dominating the sea". Since the tower has five storeys, it is also known as the Five-Storey Tower.

The tower measures 28 metres high, 31 metres wide and 16 metres deep. Its upturned eaves prominently protrude and its brackets are exquisitely and beautifully inserted between the top of the columns and crossbeams. The red ochre walls tastefully set off by the green glaze tiles render a grandiose and majestic view to the outlook of the tower.

After the initial construction of the tower, it suffered numerous natural and man-made calamities and underwent repeated repairs. During the final renovation in 1928, its wooden floors were turned into reinforced concrete ones and the tower was then taken up as a museum. Upon the establishment of New China, it was re-named as Guangzhou Museum. The antithetical couplet hanged inside the tower tells about the developments and vicissitudes of the tower.

Zhenghai Tower in Splendid China is reproduced on the scale of 1:15. Its glaze-tile roof top and red walls are vivid and really true to the real image.

Foshan Ancestral Temple

Located in Foshan city to the south of Guangzhou, Ancestral Temple, then known as North God Temple, was a Taoist temple built in the reign of Yuan Feng in the eleventh century of Northern Song Dynasty. It was renovated in the fifth year of Hong Wu's reign in Ming Dynasty (1372). Since the temple has a long history and plays a leading role among all the temples in Guangdong province, it is called Ancestral Temple.

The temple is rectangular in shape and covers a floor area of 3,000 square metres. It is arrayed parallel to the south and north axis, gradually rising from south to north and it consists of screen wall, Wanfu Terrace, courtyard, Lingying Memorial Arch, Jinxiang Pond, the Drum and Bell Towers, the Gateway, the Front Hall, the Main Hall and Zhenqing Tower. The architectural design of the temple is noted for its plain style and compact structure. Its main entrance is at the two sides of the gateway, a clever layout different from the other temples.

The Main Hall of Ancestral Temple is the chief architecture, splendid and majestic. The entire roof stands on a framework of wooden brackets in various shapes of lotus flowers, swallows and human heads interlocking with each other. They are made from the hardwood and put together without using a single nail. The construction is so exquisitely designed, firm and solid and hence it retains its own unique characteristics among other architectures.

Ancestral Temple has been celebrated as the treasure house of artistic sculptures. The entire building is extensively decorated with various kinds of exquisite sculptures such as stone inscriptions, lime-sculptures, pottery figures, brick-carvings, wood-carvings as well as iron and bronze-castings. Such a superb collection of beautiful exhibits really gives one a great and artistic treats. The giant Tortoise-Snake Stone Sculpture as imposingly crouches on Jinxiang Pond absolutely wins the admiration of all. On the 100-metre-long eaves of this building are the 2,000 pieces of famous Shiwan sculptured human figures in 24 batches that are marvellously and exquisitely designed, with lively and vivid facial expressions fully symbolizing the outstanding masterpiece in the ceramic art history.

The huge wood sculpture of "Li Yuanba Taming the Wild Horse" in the Main Hall, the 5,000-odd jin bronze statue of North God at the Front Hall together with the pottery sculptures on the ridges of the building roof are rated as the "Three Uniquenesses" in Ancestral Temple.

Ancestral Temple in Splendid China is reproduced on the scale of 1:15. The tiny sculptures on the building roof are designed and inlaid by the Shiwan Ceramic Arts Plant with new-style composition and layout possessing a unique artistic features of its own.

Tengwang Tower

Located on Ganjiang River in Nanchang city of Jiangxi province, Tengwang Tower was built in 659 by the King Teng, Li Yuanying, the younger brother of Emperor Daizhong of Tang Dynasty, when he was stationed here as an army commander. It gained fame after Wang Bo, a famous poet of Tang Dynasty, wrote the masterpiece "Eulogy to Tengwang Tower". Since then the tower has become popular and been admired by later generations.

During the past one thousand years, Tengwang Tower was destroyed and rebuilt for many times. The scale is different in different dynasties. The tallest one was three-storey building, 29.7 metres high, 28.4 metres long from west to east and 14.8 metres wide from north to south. There are two pavilions, one is called Yajiang in the south and other, Yicui in the north. Later Ying'en Pavilion was added to be built. This was the place where emperors announced edicts or bestowed gifts to officers. On the top of the pavilion are written various poems in praise, inscriptions and drawings passing on generations to generations. The words "The best pavilion in Xijiang" are written on the top of the front hall. At the back hall, the inscriptions written by Han Yu in ancient style of calligraphy are "There are many beautiful scenes in southern China, and Tengwang Tower is the best. It is the most magnificent tower with its unique feature". On its horizontal bar, the words" The old home of celestial being" are written on it.

In recent years, Tengwang Tower has been rebuilt and renovated. The scale and the grandeur is not inferior to its prime.

The Tengwang Tower in Splendid China is reproduced on the scale of 1:15. With its grandeur and antiquity, the tower still preserves its unique artistic style of ancient architecture.

The Temple of Goddess of the Sea

At present, there are more than one thousand Temples of Goddess of the Sea distributed in different places of the world. People of various nationalities worship the Goddess of the Sea — Lin Mo, whose hometown is located on Meizhou Island in Putian county, Fujian province.

It is said that Lin Mo was born in the time of the Five Dynasties (907-960). She rescued a lot of fishermen and merchant ships on the sea in her lifetime. To thank for her benevolence, people set up a temple to worship her on the island and called it "Ma Zu Temple". This custom was gradually followed in Taiwan, Southeast Asia and other places in the world. The "Ma Zu Temple" on Meizhou Island was built in A.D. 987, consisting of five architectural complexes with carved beams and painted pillars, decorated brilliantly. In A.D. 1374, more buildings were built around the temple, such as "Sleeping Hall", "Worshipping Hall", "Drum Tower", gate to the temple, etc. In A.D. 1683, the temple was rebuilt and enlarged by adding two new buildings to it, "Bell and Drum Tower" as well as "Dressing and Making-up Hall", majestic and magnificent. Facing the sea with tidewater rising and falling and the sound of the roaring waves echoing in the air, the temple looks more charming and beautiful. On 23rd of March in Chinese lunar calendar, Ma Zu's birthday, a large number of Taiwan compatriots and worshippers from various countries come to worship the Goddess of the Sea or have a sightseeing on the island, and an unprecedented grand occasion is seen here.

The Temple of Goddess of the Sea in Splendid China is reproduced on the scale of 1:15. It preserves to the full the characteristics of the ancient architectural style of southern Fujian. When tourists come to this place, the scene brings back their memories and makes them long for their homeland and ancestors.

Natural Scenery

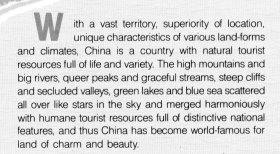

With a vast territory, superiority of location, unique characteristics of various land-forms and climates, China is a country with natural tourist resources full of life and variety. The high mountains and big rivers, queer peaks and graceful streams, steep cliffs and secluded valleys, green lakes and blue sea scattered all over like stars in the sky and merged harmoniously with humane tourist resources full of distinctive national features, and thus China has become world-famous for land of charm and beauty.

Tianshan Mountains

Tianshan Mountains, like a long dragon, stretch over the middle part of Xinjiang 1,000-odd kilometres from west to east and 300 kilometres from south to north. Their mountain ranges overlap one after another, wriggling and undulating, presenting an imposing and grandiose view. People used to call them "the White-Headed Mountains". They are 5,445 metres above sea level and their peaks are perennially snow-capped, hence the name, "the Sea of Snow". The continuous and unbroken snow-capped peaks, sparklingly silvery, tower aloft into the blue sky and they are also described as "mountains like the jades in multitude" in ancient books. The fantastic mountains have endless charm giving rise to different majestic phenomena: Sometimes it seems that the turbulent sea of clouds cluster round them. Or at times, a thin veil of misty clouds embraces them like a veiled Uygur girl vaguely displaying her charming face that it looks all the more lovely and mysterious. Due to the geographical location of Tianshan Mountains at the north-west part, the stones effloresce in a quicken speed and therefore grotesque rocks stand in great numbers, some like elephants, some like roosters, miraculous, rich and colourful.

The hidden primitive forest of Tianshan Mountains is the place abundant with forest resources. The lofty and thick mountains also serve as the habitat for the rare birds and animals. The valuable medicinal materials such as pilose antler, antelope's horn, edible lark's nest and snow lotus are all produced in these immense forest and snowfield. Tianshan Mountains are so fertile and abundant that they prove themselves to be "the Treasure Mountains" in Xinjiang.

Mount Taishan

M t. Taishan, called Daishan or Daizhong in the old days, was changed its name into "Taishan Mountain" in the time of Spring and Autumn Period. The main peak of Mt. Taishan, known as Yuhuang (Jade Emperor) Peak, lying in Tai'an county, rises 1,524 metres above sea level. The peak pierces the skies with great momentum. You can see centuries-old pines and cypresses, gurgling springs and falls, and deep ravines everywhere. On the top of the mountain, you can witness nature's kaleidoscopic changes: sunrise in the morning, coloured glow in the evening, the golden strip of the Yellow River below, and the bright moon floating on a sea of clouds — these are known as "the Four Wonders". As the scenes are changeable in four seasons, it ranks first in magnificence among the "five sacred mountains of China." In ancient times, many feudal rulers of various dynasties, deified and visited Mt. Taishan to attend grand sacrificial ceremonies. Through the years, poets, scholars and men of letters visited this sacred mountain, and left behind countless inscriptions and calligraphies. Li Bai, a great poet of Tang Dynasty, was inspired to write the lines

in praise of Mt. Taishan, "Looking around on top of pinnacle, all eight corners under the sky are in view."

The Daimiao Temple is the first relic in the middle path of Taishan Mountain as well as the place where ancient emperors held sacrificial ceremonies before climbing up the mountain. With an area of 96,000 square metres, the temple is magnificent and ancient trees tower to the skies. Climbing up the north from Daimiao Temple, then entering the First Gate to Heaven Arch and the Halfway Gate to Heaven, the scenes vary so much that every step upward is rewarded by a fresh view. This experience can only be shared by those who have personally climbed it. Going upward from Halfway Gate to Heaven and passing through Guest Welcoming Pine, Wudafu Pines, Opposing Pines Mountain and Becoming Immortal Arch, the hardest stretch of journey to summit — the Eighteen Mountain Bends begins from here. Flanked by sheer precipitous and steep rocks, there is a skyscraping scaling ladder in the middle. If you go up the mountain, it becomes steeper and steeper. And then if you look back at the foot of the hill, you will feel as if you were really rising yourself

in the sky. From the east of South Gate to Heaven, passing Heaven Street, White-Cloud Cave and Lotus Peak, You will come to Azure Cloud Temple built in Song Dynasty. The tiles on the roof, the bells hanging from the eaves and mythological animal decorations of the main hall are all made of bronze, while the chambers on both sides are roofed with iron tiles. The Bell and Drum Tower, together with the God Gate, with their unique style, artistic layout and great variety of building materials used, has formed a magnificent high-mountain architectural complex. The life-like bronze statue of the "Goddess of the Azure Cloud" in the main hall is excellently cast.

"Thus I'll climb up to the summit and see the mountains around and below are wee." Climbing up the top of Jade Emperor Peak, the scenery is beyond description: gazing into the distance shrouded by white clouds rising from below, the rolling mountains floating on a sea of clouds just beneath your feet. It is really a spectacular sight and the Heavenly Pillar Peak is worth for its name. There are Jade Emperor Palace, Sun Watching Pavilion, etc. on it. Below the Sun Watching Peak in its southeast, there is a megalith stretching out from the level ground for as far as more than twenty feet, which is called the Congbai Rock. Here is the best place for watching sunrise in the distant East China Sea.

Three Gorges of the Changjiang River

O n the upper reaches of the Changjiang River, there is a narrow, magnificent gorge with sheer precipices on both sides. This is the world-famous "Three Gorges of the Changjiang River". Extending 193 kilometres from Fengjie of Sichuan in the west to Yichang of Hubei in the east, the Three Gorges — Qutangxia Gorge, Wuxia Gorge and Xilingxia Gorge are widely known for their breathtaking beauty, magnificent, precipitous peaks and mountain cliffs, deep, fascinating valleys and whirling rapids.

The Qutangxia Gorge, also called Kui Gorge, extends from the White King Shrine in the west to the town of Daixizhen in the east, with a total length of eight kilometres. The Qutangxia Gorge, the first gorge, is the shortest but the grandest of the three. Sheer precipices on either side are less than a hundred metres apart and form a colossal, nearly a perfect gate over the river, presenting the most spectacular scene.

Following the Qutangxia Gorge is the 40-kilometre-long Wuxia Gorge where the river snakes between 1,000-metre-high cliffs. The most spectacular are the Twelve Peaks of Wushan and the most fascinating perhaps is the Goddess Peak, named for its form as a graceful nymph.

Next is the 76-kilometre-long Xilingxia Gorge in the east, crossing Zigui and Yichang in Hubei province. Xilingxia Gorge was once feared for its perilous, treacherous shoals. Around the last bend of Xilingxia Gorge stretches a vast plain. The river suddenly becomes as wide as two thousand metres. Its water gleams in the sun like a silk ribbon in the breeze, while the sails of vessels on the river are like white flowers under a blue sky.

Huangguoshu Falls

eople are carried away with the beauty of the majestic, gorgeous and changeable waterfalls, but Huangguoshu Falls on Baishui River in Zhengning county, Guizhou province is more exciting and marvellous.

With a height of 74 metres and a width of 81 metres, the main fall rushes straight down from the top of the cliff into the Rhinoceros Pool, the vapour splashed reaches as high as 90 metres. When the torrent rushes down turbulently, its roar resounds like landslide or thunder rumbling through the sky. When the sun shines on the water drops, there appears a spectacular array of rainbows in the air. What a fascinating scene!

Behind the main fall on the precipice 40 metres above the Rhinoceros Pool, there is a natural cave, the Water Curtain Cave. When you watch the fall from inside, the flood pouring down from above forms a silver curtain hanging in front of the cave. Looking up from the entrance, you feel as if the water were coming down from the sky. Such a unique scene is really matchless. The falls ranks first in China and is one of the most splendid of its kind in the world.

At the foot of the falls is jade-green Rhinoceros Pool, which is 17.7 metres deep. Legend has it that a rhinoceros once crawled out of this pool — an unlikely story, but the name has stuck. As the water roars into the pool, foam rises fifty to sixty metres, water mingling with mist and shimmering in the sunlight. Rainbows occur frequently at sunset in summer, appearing as colourful bridges above the clouds. So concentrated and varied are the waterfalls in Huangguoshu that they are rarely seen in other parts of the world. Huangguoshu Falls is a unique scenic spot consisting mainly of waterfalls, caves and stone forests. It certainly is "one of the marvellous vistas in China", true to the name.

Scenery of Lijiang

 ijiang River originates from the northeast part of Xing'an county in Guilin, Guangxi. It meanders along Guilin, Yanghsuo and converges into Xijiang in Wuzhou. The river flows for 40 kilometres from Guilin to Yangshuo and it is full of natural scenery of queer peaks and clear water. Not only are there beautiful sceneries of jutting green peaks reflecting on water which are amicable to each other and rows of peasant sheds as well as numerous fishing boats sailing on water, but also thick bamboo forests and a vast expanse of enchanting farmland. Such a picturesque landscape is presented along the waterway.

The scenery of Lijiang River is reputed as the fairyland in the world. Along both banks of the river, weirdly shaped hills stand in great numbers with limpid water surrounding. Green peaks seem afloating on water and such wonderful scenery composes a beautiful landscape of a hundred li in length. Everywhere on the river, you may find it worth repeating the words of the famous poem written by Han Yu of Tang Dynasty — "The river is like a green silk ribbon, while the hills are emerald hairpins." Taking a pleasure boat ride along the passable water route of Guilin and Yangshuo, you can see through thousands upon thousands of peculiar peaks and at the same time, the panoramic view of Guilin and Yangshuo is all within eyesight. So charming and picturesque the scenery of Lijiang River is, it thus becomes the famous scenic spot in China.

Lunan Stone Forest

The Stone Forest, located at Lunan Yi Nationality Autonomous county, 120 kilometres southeast of Kunming city, is one of the famous scenic spots in China. Covering an area of more than 400,000 mu, of which 1,000 mu, the most exquisite area of the stone forest is open to visitors. The height of the stone peaks and rock pillars is from several metres to thirty or forty metres and queer mountains and famous springs are found everywhere. Lunan Stone Forest is the largest one among its kinds in the world. In the stone forest, you will see jagged rocks of grotesque shapes and numerous fantastic peaks in different poses and full of variety, majestic and magnificent. The stone forest is thus reputed as the "Number One Grand Spectacle on Earth".

The stone peaks are scattered all over like stars in the place. Ridges and peaks rise one after another and stone forests stretch for miles and miles. A great number of perilous peaks are in different poses. There are too many things coming into sight that your eyes are kept fully occupied. There is a stretch of lawn with an area of dozens of mu in the stone forest. In spring and autumn, the mountain flowers are luxuriantly blooming everywhere. On June 24th of every lunar year, the local Sani people celebrate their national festival, the Torch Festival. In the day time, traditional performances like wrestling, pole-climbing, horsemanship and marksmanship are going on excitedly. When the land is enveloped in a curtain of night, the young people are singing and dancing merrily around the bonfire till far into the night. Ashima Stone Peak standing at the bank of the blue pool is the most famous one among them. As the legend goes, in the resistance against the local despot, Rebubala who forced her to marry his son, Ashima together with Ahe fought against him and finally they escaped from the dangerous situation. When they arrived at this place, Rebubala, colluding with the "God of Cliff", turned the place into a fierce flood and Ashima was drowned by it. Later, she turned into a huge rock erecting imposingly at the very place. This beautiful, moving love story of Ashima has spread far and wide among the masses in Yunnan for more than a thousand years. It has been written into long poem in praise of the heroine.

According to the recorded history, as early as 300 years ago, people already visited the stone forest. Sun Peng once wrote a poem "The Song of Stone Forest" praising its extraordinary sight during the years of Kang Xi's reign in Qing Dynasty. The ten most appealing scenes in the stone forest named by people of modern times are Splendid Scenery of Stone Forest, A Narrow Gap between Two Cliffs, Phoenix Making Up Its Wings, Viewing the Peak from the Pavilion, Ashima Stone Peak, Sunset Glow at Stone Gate, Feeding the Baby Bird, Guanyin Coming up out of Water, Mother and Son Strolling Side by Side and Elixir Mushroom. Here you will enjoy the peculiar sight of the countless stone peaks assuming a thousand different shapes, all fanciful and picturesque. You will be dazzled by the enchanting sight as if you were in the fairyland.

Five-Finger Mountain and "Heaven's Limit and Sea's Margin"

ainan Island, the glittering pearl in South China Sea, was in ancient times known as "Ya" prefecture or "Qiong" Island. The blue sea, the coconut groves, the evergreen trees and the unwithered flowers make up a picturesque landscape of tropical flavour of this island.

Along the middle part of the island lies the Wuzhishan (Five-Finger) Mountain whose five verdant peaks are towering and stretching from southwest to northeast like the outstretched five fingers. The highest among the five fingers is the forefinger which measures at 1,879 metres above sea level and 347 metres taller than Taishan Mountain. A gorge "serene and of delicate beauty" is located between the thumb and the index finger. The middle finger, the ring finger and the little finger are meandering but connecting with each other depicting a vast expanse of boundless fresh green. The mountain also functions as the watershed for the Wan Quan River, matching with the scene of "clear and limpid mountain streams". Climbing up the Wuzhishan Mountain, one will appreciate a sensation of "white clouds floating past right before one's eyes and light mists rising under one's feet". Besides, one can experience the weather condition of "four seasons in one day", that is, cool in the morning, hot in the afternoon, warm in the evening and cold at night. Therefore, they become the themes for the men of letters of all ages to recite poetry or to portray drawings.

Qiu Ling, the great scholar of Ming Dynasty, at his age of thirteen wrote a famous poem praising the towering, precipitous and magnificent Wuzhishan Mountain.

Hainan Island was previously used as the remotest place of exile for convicts. Cheng Zhe, a prefecture magistrate of Ya prefecture during Yong Zheng's reign in Qing Dynasty inscribed at the then chief mountain pass, now the location to the west of Port Sanya, the words "Heaven's Limit and Sea's Margin." Here the tropical rain forest is dense and thick, heaps of peculiar rocks scattering in the surrounding, and the sound of the rippling waves and tides heard time and again. All these give one the taste of "rosy clouds coming down from the sky, fresh breeze blowing from the sea".

Seven-Star Crags

The seven magnificent and steep crags prominently erecting themselves one after another like the Big Dipper stand aloft over the blue and limpid waters. With its grotesque crags, fantastic caves and beautiful lakes, the Seven-Star Crags possess 7 crags, 8 caves, 5 lakes and 6 hillocks and have long been reputed as a wonderful place boasting picturesque scenery of "the hills in Guilin and the waters in Hangzhou". The seven crags from east to west are respectively named: Langfeng (the Wind from the Space), Jade Screen, Stone Chamber, Heavenly Pillar, Toad, Stone Palm and Abo. The Stone Chamber Cave under the Stone Chamber Crag and the Double-Opening Cave beneath the Abo Crag draw many visitors' attention to see their magnificent

stalacites which appear in the shapes of peculiar birds and beasts, figures, mountains and rivers as well as flowers and trees. They look like the fierce lion, the crawling tortoise, an agile mouse, a flight of birds returning to their nests, the lotus flowers in full bloom, the miraculous cactus, the giant dragon wriggling with claws stretching out and seems to rise high in the sky and their appearances and shapes are vivid and really true to life. The lake goes deep into the cave and a lamplit boat trip in the caves is a memorable experience. All these crags lean against the cliff to the north and the other three sides are encircled by the lake water. The Star Lake covers a total area of 460 hectares and is crisscrossed by causeways to form 5 big lakes. The 20-odd-kilometre-long causeways are densely

planted with weeping willows and trees and they connect to the green shades of hillocks. The silver lakes and the green hills add radiance and beauty to each other and the whole area is made much more charming and attractive like a fairyland.

Moon-in-the-water Palace, located to the southern cliff of Stone Chamber Crag, originally known as Bodhisattva Hall, is the biggest temple in Seven-Star Crags. It faces the Star Lake in the front and leans against the strange peaks at the rear and the grandiose palace hall is tastefully set off by the red walls and the green tiles. The main hall is connected with the other building structures by the winding verandas. The whole complex stands simple and unsophisticated but solemn and majestic with outline exquisitely designed. The four sides of the main hall are covered with thickly planted trees and luxuriant flowers. This couples with the surrounding picturesque scenery, so natural and enchanting, and thus it is worthy of its name — Moon-in-the-water Palace.

Xiqiao Mountain

Xiqiao Mountain in Nanhai county is one of the two best-known mountains in Guangdong province and it has long been famed for its picturesque scenery. Covering a total area of 20 square kilometres, the mountain comprises 8 mountain villages, 72 peaks, 36 caves and 21 crags. Over 200 clear running springs scatter around the whole scenic resort, thus it enjoys other reputation as the "Spring Mountain". There are 28 flying waterfalls also found in the scenic spot. Among them Yuyanzhukeng Waterfall, the Thousand-foot-high Waterfall, Yunyan Waterfall, Yunlutiequan Waterfall are the four most fascinating ones in Xiqiao Mountain.

There are many tourist attractions in the mountain area but the surroundings of Baiyun Cave in the western part are the essence of all the beautiful scenery. People used to say: "If you want to take a tour of Mt. Xiqiao, you should first visit Baiyun Cave." As legend goes, Ho Baiyun, a scholar of Ming Dynasty made friends and studied here, hence the name Baiyun Cave. Here, Yunquan Immortal Hall, Kuiguang Tower, White Cloud Ancient Temple, Three Lakes Academy, etc. form the famous group of architecture which are of primitive simplicity and exquisitely constructed. Thick and green Banyan trees, hardy and old pines as well as the brilliant red azalea surround the whole area. The air is heavy with the aroma of the orange osmanthus against the backdrop of the mirror-like ponds. Cliffs seem to be hanged in the air. Water keeps dripping from the springs on the hillsides and pavilions and towers are built amid the forest of pines and cypresses. The scenery is charming and beautiful forming a distinctive and famous scenic spot.

At the eastern and middle part of the scenic area, clear springs, grotesque rocks, fantastic crags and bizarre caves such as Tuming Cave, Boshi Cave, Nine Dragons Cave, etc. all have unique and tasteful beauty. The most peculiar of all is the Stone Swallow Cave which is big and spacious enough to accommodate a few hundred people. By the right side of the cave steeply rises a giant screen. The cave is full of water all the year round, mysterious, deep and serene. Countless stone swallows circle around overhead mirroring in the water to become an integrated mass. One is hard to distinguish the real swallows from the inverted ones reflected in water. Such a scene is marvellous and appealing to tourists.

Alishan Mountain Scenic Spot and Yehliu Park in Taiwan

Taiwan's famous Alishan Mountain Scenic Spot, located in the northeast of Jiayi city, consists of 18 mountains, such as Dawuluanshan Mountain, Jianshan Mountain, Zhushan Mountain, Tashan Mountain, etc. The highest peak is 2,905 metres above sea level. The whole scenic spot covers an area of about 175 hectares.

The four most wonderful scenes in Alishan Mountain Scenic Spot are: 1. The magnificent sea of clouds. When ascending a height to enjoy a distant view in fine weather, you can see the sea of clouds getting thicker and thicker floating on the mountains and in the valleys. Sometimes they look like a vast ocean with the dashing of billows, sometimes they look like the white snow piling up in the valleys, full of variety and grandeur. 2. The immense forest with soaring trees. The dense forest, evergreen all year round, with exotic trees and flowers, forms an ocean in green. 3. The wonderful scene of sunrise. Climbing the Sun-watching Tower on the top of Zhushan Mountain, you can see the contour of Jade Mountain in a distance, which reveals itself clearer and clearer in the first rays of morning sun. 4. The crimson cherries. In March and April, all over the mountains are covered with crimson cherries in blossom. "When spring comes, the mountains are covered with bright red cherries, and everywhere crowds of people are found admiring them."

The Yehliu Park famed for its fantastic rock formations, situated in Wanli village of Taipei county, is a part of Dadun Mountain Range stretching into the sea and sculptured into various forms of queer rocks due to the erosion of wind and sea over long years. Numerous huge rocks assuming different peculiar shapes formed by the constant wash of the waves are found everywhere. Among them, the most conspicuous one is the "Head of the Queen", which is most lifelike, especially its crown and the five sense organs, graceful and elegant. If you sit on the rocks near "Female Celestial Shoe" or "Lovers Rock" watching the blue sea with turbulent waves in a distance, you will be lost in admiration of the beauty of the scene.

Huangshan Mountain

Huangshan Mountain, known as Yishan Mountain in Qin Dynasty, was renamed in the sixth year of Tianbao in Tang Dynasty (A.D. 747) because the legendary Emperor Huangdi made his pills of immortality here. Huangshan Mountain covers an area of 250 square kilometres of which 154 square kilometres are scenic spots. It is reputed as the most celebrated sightseeing area both at home and abroad.

A noted Chinese traveller praised Huangshan Mountain by these words: "No mountains are worth seeing when you have travelled the Five Mountains, while the Five Mountains are nothing if you've seen Huangshan Mountain". Also, Li Bai, a famous poet in Tang Dynasty compared Huangshan Mountain as the beautiful golden lilies in full bloom by saying: "The full four thousand feet of Huangshan, the two and thirty lotus peaks. Rock pillars shooting up to kiss empyrean roses, like so many lilies grown amid a sea of gold".

Huangshan Mountain gathers tens of hundreds of queer peaks and among them 72 peaks in various sizes are in the scenic areas, of which 30 are the famous ones. The three chief peaks—Lianhua (Lotus), Tiandu (Celestial City) and Guangmingding (Bright Top) all stand over 1,800 metres above sea level. They are majestic, precipitous, peculiar and grandiose presenting a rare scene of splendour and magnificence.

The lofty and imposing peaks, the deep and serene valleys coupled with the ever-changing sea of clouds add a mysterious shade to Huangshan Mountain. From ancient times to the present, "the Four Ultimate Beauties of Huangshan Mountain" have been used to describe the peculiar features of this natural picture. The towering peaks reach into the clouds unfolding in all their majesty. The green pines, verdant and luxuriant, stand tall and straight displaying an infinite variety of exquisite beauties in pose. When clouds set in, they are like endless waves, one following another and it presents a vast expanse of sea. The grotesque rocks, spreading all over the place, rise abruptly, absolutely lifelike. The hot springs, colourless and odourless, spout all the year round, are suitable for drinking and bathing. Thus, strange pines, grotesque rocks, a sea of clouds and hot springs are widely acclaimed as "the Four Ultimate Beauties of Huangshan Mountain".

"Huangshan epitomizes the earth's most fantastic mountains and scenery". Huangshan Mountain wholly reflects the virtues of the mountains under the heaven. It possesses the distinguished features of other famous mountains — the magnificence of Taishan Mountain, the precipitousness of Huashan Mountain, the mists and clouds of Hengshan Mountains, the cataracts of Lushan Mountain, the gracefulness and the pleasant coolness of Mount Emei and the grotesque rocks of Yangdang Mountain.

Scenery of West Lake

the place more fascinating. Su Dongpou, the famous poet of Song Dynasty eulogized the lake by comparing it with the ancient Chinese beauty named Xi Zi who looked equally attractive either with or without make-up. The poet spoke for all when he wrote the following lines:

Shimmering, sparkling, sun-drenched Lake,
All beauty to the view;
Far hills, mist-shrouded, glimpsed through showers,
Are as enchanting, too.
Men say no jewels or robes enhanced
The Beauty of Xi Zi;
And West Lake, decked or unadorned,
May well compare with her.

The ten scenic spots of West Lake initially appeared in the title of a short artistic creation by an artist in Southern Song Dynasty.

The existing ten sceneries are Dawn at the Sun Dyke in Spring Time, Autumn Moon on Calm Lake, Watching Fish at the Bending Flower Stream, Orioles Warbling amongst the Weeping Willows, Double Peaks Shooting up to the Clouds, Three Pools Mirroring the Moon, Sunset Scene at Lei Peak, Evening Bell at Nan Ping, Lotus in the Summer Breeze in Qu Garden and Remnant Snow on the Broken Bridge. These sceneries all wear a new look different from the ones in Song Dynasty.

West Lake was first named as Wulin Water, Qiantang Lake and Western Fairy Lake. Hemmed in on three sides by water, the lake faces the city proper on one side. Lying in the west of Hangzhou city of Zhejiang province, the lake began to be called West Lake in Song Dynasty. The lake, almost ellipse in shape, covers an area of 6.03 square kilometres. The surface area of water occupies 5.2 square kilometres with a circumference of 15 kilometres. Its bottom is quite even and its average depth being 1.5 metres, the deepest at 2.8 metres and the shallowest at 1 metre. It is divided into five parts — the Outer Lake, the Inner Lake, Yue Lake, Xi Li Lake and Lesser South Lake by two dykes, the Bai Dyke and Su Dyke. Located in the middle of the lake are the Solitary Hill, Miniature Fairyland, Mid-Lake Pavilion and Ruan Yuan's Mound. Golden Sand Port, Long Hong Gully and Long Bridge Stream are the main streams flowing into the lake whereas Shen Tang Sluice Gate meandering through Sheng Tang River into the canal as well as Yong Jin Sluice Gate flowing through the underground tube of Huan Sha River into the urban river outside Wulin Gate, are the two outlets to regulate the flow of the lake water. West Lake in its prehistoric days, connecting to Qiantang River, was a shallow bay. Later, sludge began to deposit on the bed of the bay separating the sea, hence the inland water at the sandspit became a lake. Being washed by mountain springs and running water with successive artificial dredging and harnessing, and the ingenious combination of nature and man-power, this lake has become world-famous. West Lake, the hub on the 49-square-kilometre scenery park, are scattered with more than 40 scenic sites and over 30 major historical reclics. Chains of mountains pile up one after another against the background of luxuriant flowers and trees. Springs, pools, creeks and brooks are weaving through their ways among peaks, crags, caves and gullies. Verdant and dark green trees with pavilions, pagodas and grottoes all help to make

Folk Customs and Dwellings

G eographically China is one of the biggest countries in the world. The ancient country boasts about 56 nationalities living in compact communities and working together in a beautiful and richly endowed land with an area of 9.6 million square kilometres and thus creating China's splendid culture with a long history. Different nationalities and different regions bring about colourful customs and habits as well as varied festive activities. Similarly, the houses in which people are living have, from types to shapes, plenty of variety and unique characteristics.

Quadrangle

uadrangle is a kind of compound houses in Beijing. The standard compound faces south or north and the gate is not exactly in the middle. There is a screen wall, courtyard, main room and side rooms inside the gate. The wall on both sides of the gate is rectangular or square. With the gate closed, the compound is a very secure family. People called it "Siheyuan".

Here is one of the group of compounds in Mao'er Alley of Dongcheng District in Beijing. The big mansion to its north was the residence of Queen Wan Rong of the last dynasty. People called it "Goddess Mansion". The Queen celebrated her birthday on the 29th of the ninth month of the lunar year in 1922 before she was taken into the palace. The gateway was richly decorated, and the courtyard was thronged with visitors. High-ranking officials and officers all came to celebrate the grand occasion.

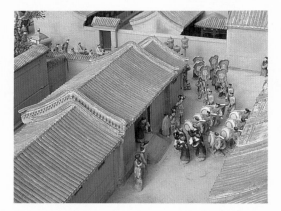

The Bai Dwelling Houses

Dali, an ancient city of the Bai Autonomous Region in Yunnan province, is the place mostly inhabited by the Bai people. Their dwelling houses are varied in forms and the typical layout of the Bai architecture is called "Three-Room House". It is composed of a two-storey main building and a separately built kitchen and livestock farm. These three rooms, which have small courtyards in between, serving different uses, are constructed with brick walls, wooden framework and thatched roof top. The upper floor of the main building is used to store up grain and food. The ground floor is for living quarters. Cooking is done in the kitchen whereas the livestock farm is only for raising animals.

The two-storey wooden thatched house, the bamboo-and-wood structured house and the house with stone walls, wooden framework and thatched roof are three kinds of houses for the Bai people in mid-level mountain area. For those who are living in the frigid mountain region, the transverse wood segments are piled up to form the "wood-stack house" comprising either single room or link-up double rooms. In order to keep away from coldness and keep warm, a brazier which burns perennially is made in the room for warming and cooking in the daytime and lighting at night. Besides, the whole family sleep on the floor surrounding the brazier.

The Bai people are good at singing and dancing and they live a rich and colourful life. On festive night, the whole village is brightly lit up with bonfire and the villagers are immersed in the merry soft music and graceful dances.

Mongolian Yurt

The Mongolian people have been for generations adopting the nomadic-type of living in the grasslands and moving from place to place in search of water and grass. Mongolian yurts, the unique dwelling houses, are under such circumstances being constructed for the Mongolians to adopt to such a way of living.

The Mongolian yurt is set up by the supporting pillar in the centre of the circle from where extending out to a large circle of three to four metres. The roof top, appearing in dome-shape, is formed by a framework of wooden slats, measuring at a height of three to five metres. A movable wall on top of the circumference of the roof is tied up with the willow meshes and is covered on top with reeds in summer and camel skin or thick fur carpet in winter. Its only door is open to the south with an opening at the top. The floor inside the yurt is furnished with fur blankets and the walls are covered with snow-white silk fabric, warm and comfortable.

Mongolian yurts are easy to dismantle, transport and set up depending upon seasonal changes and are especially made for the requirements of the nomadic lifestyle. Its circular exterior is exempted from being blown down by the strong wind in the grassland. Moreover, its umbrella-shaped roof top accumulates no rain or snow providing the most suitably movable dwellings for the herdsmen.

"Nadam" is a Mongolian word meaning "amusement" or "games". Nadam Fair, a traditional festival of Mongolians, is celebrated in July and August each year. Many thousands of herdsmen in gala dress make their way to the spot where the fair takes place on horse-back from all directions with portable Mongolian yurts and camels with full cart-loads to join the festive occasion. The grassland, a serene place at normal times, is now packed with close and numerous Mongolian yurts. Tents are put up as makeshift shops to display vast collection of commodities. Traditional horseracing, wrestling and Mongolian song and dance are performed at the same time to add a bustling and jubilant atmosphere to the festival.

The model of the Mongolian yurt in Splendid China is really true to life. Its outlook is bright-coloured and beautiful and it forms a contrast to the lovely view against the backdrop of the green grass, flowers, peculiar pines and verdant cypresses. The vivid and lifelike pottery figurines are placed before the Mongolian yurt in the grassland. Some portray the images of celebrating the Nadam Fair with the performance of singing and dancing. Others listen with rapt attention to the plucking of the bow-stringed musical instrument. The wrestlers march and dance into the arena, standing in full battle array for the fight. The grand fair in which the Mongolian yurt mixing with the lively pottery figurines makes up a beautiful and lovely picture.

Cave Dwelling in Northern Shaanxi

ave Dwelling, the traditional living place in northwest of loess plateau, is widely distributed at the middle and upper reaches of Huanghe River. The area of it is about 600,000 square kilometres and the population living in it is about 40 million.

The cave has three kinds of structures: stone, brick and earth. All caves are built at the foot of the mountain or at the side of the cliff. Usually each cave is 5 to 7 metres long, 3 to 4 metres wide and over 3 metres high. It faces south and its door and windows are on the south side. The solid earth of 2 metres thick on the cave is very strong and it is often used as a place of threshing wheat or a thoroughfare.

In a cave, a hollow heated brick bed is built near the window which is connected to the kitchen range. The smoke of cooking directly reaches the chimney on the top cave from the wall through the fire-way under the bed. In this way, it cannot only save firewood and keep warm but also keep the fresh air in a cave.

The heated brick bed is the place where the family lives a daily life, sleeps and treats the guests. The guests are invited to sit on the bed and given the best food by the hosts. This is the traditional way of treating a guest in northern Shaanxi.

By using local materials, the construction of the cave is simple and cheap. The cave is easy to be repaired but difficult to be damaged. In addition, it is heat insulated so it is warm in winter and cool in summer. The cave dwelling is indeed an ideal living place on cold loess plateau. The cave dwellings have two styles: independent style and honeycomb style in which the caves are connected to each other. A family occupies the upper half and another family the lower half. At present, the newly-built cave dwellings covered with brick or stones on its walls become more solid and beautiful.

ibin District in the south of Sichuan, famous for its picturesque scenery and the towering cliffs and precipices, was once the hometown of the ancient Bo people. Though the Bo people no longer existed and vanished without a trace, they left behind the cultural remains of cliff murals and hanging coffins.

Hanging coffin is one of the burial ritual practised by the Bo people, an ancient minority nationality. The ruins of hanging coffins and cliff murals are the most typical and largely distributed at Matangba in Gongxian, Yibin. Onto the dozen-kilometre-long cliffs and rocks, murals painted in bright red are discovered in which the subjects are very diverse and imaginative: martial arts, fencing, horse-racing, kicking shuttlecocks and dancing, reflecting the daily life of the Bo people. Apart from these, there are rivers and trees, the fierce tigers and leopards as well as the deep-water sea-monsters and fish on the murals showing the primitive religious concepts of the Bo people.

These murals, designed in a simplistic technique but outlined in an unsophisticated way with shapes vivid and themes outstanding, fully exhibit the intelligence, wisdom and cultural styles of the Bo people.

Most fascinated are the hanging coffins scattered along the dozen-kilometre-long cliffs. The bodies of the Bo people's ancestors were placed inside the hanging coffins. According to the on-the-spot written records from the experts, the coffins were hewn out from the tough nanmu and mulberry trees. Some coffins are put into the already dug-out holes or placed inside the natural rock caves; another way is to dig holes on the cliff in which wooden pillars are planted to support the coffins. The coffins sometimes are piled up one after another or arrayed triangularly. Based on statistics, 288 hanging coffins are preserved and they last for over a few hundred years. This is the typical feature of the Bo people to bury their ancestors in hanging coffins.

Cliff-Side Tombs

The Dong Village

eople of the Dong nationality are distributed in the provinces of Guizhou, Hunan and Guangxi. Each family has its own separate house. Most of the houses of the Dong on the plains are two-storey buildings in wood with outer multi-corridor style. The roofs are covered with the skin of fir or thatch. At two ends of the house, there are side buildings which look like the shape of a polygon. The houses near the rivers or on the slopes, called "tiaojiaolou", with distinctive flavour, are a kind of suspending houses with only some long poles in wood supporting the back parts of the buildings.

Whatever wooden houses or "tiaojiaolou", the downstairs room is for storing farm tools, sundries, etc. as well as penning animals. The upper floor is well ventilated. In the middle is the living room which is used for having meals and entertaining guests and the bedrooms lie on both sides. In each side room, a fire is made for warming, lighting and cooking.

In all Dong villages, there must be a drum tower. The lower part of the tower is square in shape. The tower is a multi-storey wooden structure with upturned eaves, tier upon tier, carved in pattern paintings in bright colour while the tile eaves on top of the building are polygon-shaped like a pagoda. The unique pagoda-shaped drum tower is made of fir timber. For the construction of the tower, instead of nails, intricate and precisely matched dowelling joints are devised. Some drum towers, fifteen-storey in height, look majestic and magnificent. There is a big drum made of birch wood on the top of the tower. When something important happens in the village, the clan elder beats the drum to gather the villagers, and that is why it is called drum tower.

The drum tower is not only the symbol of the Dong, but also the important place for meetings, offering sacrifices to ancestors and mediating disputes. Ordinarily, the drum tower is a good place for villagers to rest and for young poeple to talk love. When night has fallen, you can hear the continuous love songs accompanied by the melodious music coming from the ground floor of the drum tower, filling the atmosphere with love and joy.

The Wind-and-Rain Bridge

he wind-and-rain bridge is unique to the Dong people. With a style of its own, highly skilled, the bridge is the crystal of the architectural art of the Dong. Though the wind-and-rain bridges of the Dong in Guizhou are not so large and majestic as the ones in Guangxi, they are famous for their exquisite design and graceful shape.

The wind-and-rain bridges in Guizhou differ in size and style. Some are stretching over both ends of big rivers and some over streams in the villages. They facilitate communications, embellishing scenery and symbolizing "luck". In addition, they are built at the corners of the fields crossing canals, exquisite and pretty. They offer shelter against rain and sun and places for many uses as well.

Apart from the central bridge pier built in stones, the rest of the Dong's wind-and-rain bridge is all made of wood, without using a single nail or screw. An intricate hole-boring and joining system is employed in the building of the bridge, compact texture, firm and secure. It fully shows the superb technique of the Dong's artisans.

It has a pavilion at each end and centre of the wind-and-rain bridge. Ordinarily, the one in the centre is higher than the next on each side. Differing in size, the bridges are divided into different styles of three-layer eaves or five-layer eaves, 3 to 5 metres high. With upturned eaves, jutting-out corners, paintings and sculptures of rare birds and animals, the bridge is of primitive simplicity and looks beautiful. A corridor is built from end to end to link up the three pavilions on the bridge. On both sides of the inner walls of the corridor, there are coloured painting of historical stories of the Dong people, figures and scenery, flowers, birds, fishes and insects. The bridge, adorned with rich multicoloured decorations, looks gorgeous and graceful, hence the name "Multicoloured Bridge" as well.

The wind-and-rain bridge, the great creativity of the Dong people, connects not only rivers and streams in the village, but also provides shelter for passers-by against rain and sun. It is an important place for the Dong people to gather or to sing and dance together as well as a place for young people to talk love. Whenever the moon rises in the sky, the clear, limpid water and the gorgeous bridge appear before your eyes and the melodious love songs, the merry talk and laughter can be heard constantly, and all this carries you away.

The Bouyei Village

 Most of the Bouyei villages in Guizhou are located at the foot of Pingba Mountain. The houses of the Bouyei people are mainly built in wood which is produced locally. Apart from one-storey and two-storey buildings, there are "slate houses" with the roofs covered in slates, all bearing the characteristics of Bouyei nationality.

The house which most represents the distinctive national features of the Bouyei is "banbianlou" building, which is built on the slope of the mountain. The front half part is a wooden two-storey building and the back half part one-storey building. There are three rooms, five rooms, seven rooms or nine rooms in "banbianlou" building, but they are all in odd numbers. The downstairs part of the front house is used for storing goods and penning animals. The front upper part and the back part of the two-storey building are for dwelling. The middle room is a place for worshipping god and ancestors as well as entertaining guests. It is also called central room which also has a shrine for idols, under it, the ancestral tablets are placed on a square table for worshipping. The back rooms are often used as bedrooms. The side rooms on both sides of the central room are divided into kitchen, bedroom and guest room specially used for guests staying

for the night. The bedroom and the guest room are provided with heated brick beds which are connected with the cooking range of the kitchen. The arrangement of the room is plain and simple, but clean, tidy and comfortable.

The Bouyei people are good at singing and dancing. Their life is rich and colourful. After dark, with the lively, fast rhythm of bronze drumbeats, people sing and dance merrily far into the night.

To celebrate the traditional festival, the Bouyei people sing and dance happily in an open-air public square. From January 1—15, lunar calendar, men and women in best clothes from various villages, riding horses with arms, gather at the square. There are huge crowds of people in the field. Men are taking part in horse racing, archery or wrestling while women are dancing and throwing balls made of silk. The beating of gongs and drums resounds to the skies. From July 1—15, lunar calendar, there is a festival somewhat like "tiao shen" (sorcerer's dance in a trance), called "fang ba xian" (to release the Eight Immortals.) This grand gathering can be matched with the horse racing festival held in spring, both bearing strong national characteristics.

The Miao Village

 eople of the Miao nationality are largely distributed in Yunnan, Guizhou, Hunan, Hainan provinces, etc. The houses in which they are living are usually one-storey or two-storey built of wood or stones.

The Miao people in Guizhou province are mostly living in "diaojiaolou" (a wooden house supported by wooden pillars), which are projected over the hills or slopes. The houses are very distinctive in style, supported with wood pillars at four sides. The pillars at the front part are suspended from the ground, merely built for the purpose of artistic decoration, in symmetry of the pillars at the back. This can be seen the Miao craftsmen's technique of applying the principles of mechanics to architecture.

The houses are usually built of wood in two storeys or sometimes three storeys high. The ground floor is used for the storing of sundry goods, farm tools and raising animals. The first floor is spread with pieces of wooden planks and used as bedroom as well as sitting room with stove in the centre for cooking and warming in winter. In the old days, the house was very simply furnished, even without bed and the whole family was sleeping around the stove on the floor during the night. Now, most people divide their houses into two parts, sitting room and bedroom with sheet, quilt and mosquito net and the room is much better furnished.

The roof of the house is covered with the bark of China fir, locally grown. The whole village is located in a verdant and luxuriant wood of the tropics with green bamboos scattering all over the hills and slopes, and thus an extraordinary scenery of the Miao village is formed. When night is closing in, love songs are sung and reed-pipes are played, permeating with the style and features of the Miao nationality.

he bamboo-structured houses of Dai nationality in Xishuangbanna of Yunnan are small and tastefully laid out and set off by flowers and lofty trees. The house has two storeys and bamboos are commonly used for home furnishing fixtures.

The roof top of the Dai bamboo house, resembling the bottom part of the ship, is covered with the marvellous "thatch". The thatches are dried and then knitted in order on the bamboo strips. Thus, the material used is so light in weight that it cannot crush the house out of shape. Most peculiar of all is that when the sun shines on the roof top, the thatches naturally curve up to let sufficient sunshine come into the house. In case of raining, the thatches open up because of humid weather and they are closely overlapped hence creating a comfortable environment even with heavy rain.

The lower storey of the bamboo house, surrounded with bamboo fence, is used as storehouse and animal-breeding area whereas the upper storey serves as the living quarters. Corridors and flat roof for drying clothes are found outside the house, convenient and pleasing to the eye. Inside the house, it is divided into the interior part which is used as the living room and the exterior part the sitting room.

The Dai people, civilized, courteous and hospitable, develop a habit of cleanliness. Thus, it is really a pleasure to be the guest of the Dai people.

The Dai Village

A Water-Village in Southern China

 "Jiangnan is nice." "The sun rises above the river like a ball of fire, the water of the river is emerald green in spring", a poem written by Bai Ju Yi, the famous poet in Tang Dynasty eulogized the beautiful scenery of Jiangnan. Jiangnan, generally referring to Jiangsu and Zhejiang, is the place of long-standing history with prosperous culture. It is rich in

resources and people of outstanding ability come forth in large number. Apart from the above, its famous historical relics and scenic spots can be found everywhere.

Shaoxing city is one of the ancient villages in Zhejiang province. It is not only the hometown of Lu Xun, the great writer, but also one of the water villages enriched with pronounced local colour. The town lies in the environment of green hills and limpid water crisscrossed by creeks and rivers. Houses of typical features are built along the rivers with front door facing the street while the back door facing waterways. Each house has a small, narrow flagstone path leading to the river from the back door and owns its private pier. Lines of small boats lying at anchor are the indispensable water transport facilities for each household. Rows upon rows of elegantly built civilian houses in simple style strew at random along the banks, and they match with the different forms of delicate-structured stone bridges which are set off by the shuttling boats back and forth. All these form the picture of a water-village full of rich, worldly wisdom and local flavour.

Overheading building projections spanning the lane and corridor-like streets scatter all over this small village. They provide not only the shelters for passers-by either from rain or sunshine but also serve as places for the house-owners to enjoy the nearby scenery and to best communicate with the neighbours. At the centre of the village, shops, vendors' stalls, large and small restaurants as well as tea houses completely fill the streets, bustling with activity. It shows the features of "a land of fish and rice."

"San Wei School", where Lu Xun studied in his young

days, still being retained and "Xianheng Restaurant, Tugu Ancestral Hall and Linhe Stage which appeared in Lu Xun's writings add a great romantic feelings to this modern village.

Outside the village, the simple and plain houses, haystacks piled up like mountains, green trees, farmlands and rippling rivers form another view of serene and peaceful rural scenery, which makes one feel relaxed and happy.

The Dwelling Houses of the Hakkas

Yongding county in Fujian, with its picturesque scenery, is the place where the Hakkas live in clans in the unique-styled communal multi-storey building structure presenting a marvellous phenomenon and retaining a fantastic feature of its own. Its castle-like circular structure is eulogized by experts of China and foreign countries as the "world wonder" and may be rated as the uniqueness in architecture.

The circular structures, also known as Hakkas earthen buildings, are distributed in the mountain regions of Guzhu, Hukeng, Xiayang, Zhiling, etc. in Yongding county like the giant block houses, towering and in perfect array. The earthen building is designed in accordance with the concentric circle pattern from the interior to the exterior, one circle entangled with another. The outer wall is higher than the inner one, irregular but in an orderly way to build

up a circular wall in three circular layers. Each layer of the circular wall is made up of the local red earth and the outer layer measures 3 metres wide. The wall of such a building is thick at the bottom about 1.5 metres, becoming thinner to 1 metre as it rises and the whole building is in a total height of over 10 metres. The largest building is in the diameter of over 70 metres in four to five storeys but the inner wall stands lower with only one to two storeys. The building is then partitioned by brick walls or wooden planks into several rooms. The ground floor serves as kitchen, livestock farm, sundry room whereas the first floor is used to store food and the second floor is mainly living quarters. Conferences, wedding or burial ceremonies, memorial service or other activities of the clansmen are to be held in the inner circle. Except the front door installed at the outer wall, the first and

second floors are windowless. When the giant door is shut in case to keep away from the bandits, the building will simultaneously become a firm castle.

Yongding earthen building possesses virtues such as quakeproof and moistureproof. Due to its unique structure, people inside will feel warm in winter and cool in summer. Moreover, the building is solid and durable but constructed in an economical and practical way. A huge earthen building can be partitioned into three to four hundred rooms to house seventy to eighty households. Thus, since Northern Song Dynasty as the ancestors of the Hakkas moving to south China for settlement, Yongding dwelling houses of the Hakkas continued to be built and has lasted long to this day, and become the favourite dwelling houses for the Hakkas.

Chime Bells Hall

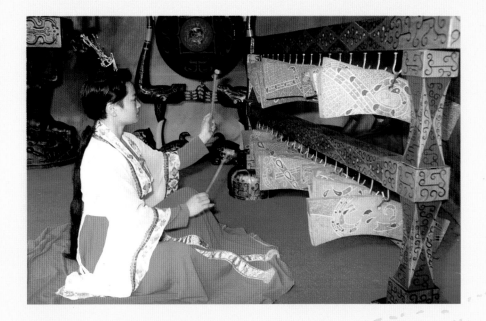

he bronze chime bells excavated from Marquis Yi's grave in the early years of Warring States Period (475-221 B.C.) was a great shock to the world. Combining archaeology, metallurgy, arts and crafts together, it is the oldest in ages, the largest in quantity and volume, the most complete in music sound and the most perfect in the technique of metallurgy. Thus, it was cited by experts at home and abroad as "the Eighth Wonder of the World".

This set of 65 pieces of chime bells were buried under the earth for more than 2,400 years, but until now they still strike the right note. The high-pitched bells send forth a sonorous pleasant sound while the base ones produce a tone that is both deep and vigorous. The complete set of serial bells, as far as the scale structure is concerned, fits into the same compass as the seven-tone scale in C major, now in wide use internationally. Its range, from the lowest to the highest pitch, covers five and a half octaves, only one octave less than that of the modern piano. Its central register is complete with the twelve semitones, which renders tonal modification extremely easy. It can play ancient and modern music, both Chinese and foreign.

The reappear of chime bells shows the brilliant culture and music of ancient China, the keynote of the music was played in the memorial ceremony and used as the symbol of social estate of the nobility. Shenzhen Splendid China Development Co., Ltd. has set up Chime Bells Hall in Splendid China Miniature Scenic Spot. In the hall, a set of 49 pieces of bronze serial bells, 32 musical instruments, such as the reed-pipe wind instrument known as the sheng, the vertical bamboo flute with a keyboard called the xiao, the horizontal bamboo flute, the 25-stringed and 7-stringed plucked instruments, the se and qin (somewhat similar to the zither), sets of serial bells and chime stones, and drums, the vertical bamboo flute xiao, the jiangu drum, the 10- and 5-stringed plucked instrument qin, 4-stringed Chinese lute, pipa, small gong, cymbals, etc. The Splendid China Chime Bells Philharmonic Orchestra plays the famous traditional Chinese music, such as "Meihuasanlong", "Chushang", "Chunjianghuayueye", etc. In addition, they also compose the chime bells song and dance and some famous foreign music. They have given nearly 2,000 showings and are highly praised and welcomed by the visitors at home and abroad. In October, 1993, the philharmonic orchestra was invited by Hong Kong Urban Council to give performance during Chinese Music Week in Hong Kong. They were praised and warmly welcomed by the audience of Hong Kong.

Through the performance of chime bells ancient music in the hall, Chinese and foreign visitors can enjoy the cream of unearthed historical and cultural relics — the huge bronze chime bells and other ancient musical instruments buried 2,400 years ago. Besides, while listening to the music of chime bells, they can have some idea of ancient China with its brilliant civilization and have a taste of customs and style of life of the State of Chu and get the same entertainment as Chinese emperors in former days.

A Street in Suzhou

In the north of Splendid China, there is a group of buildings built with white walls and grey tiles, carved beams and painted rafters in the style of Suzhou classical gardens scattering here and there, full of twists and turns. This is the world-famous "A Street in Suzhou". After visiting the "Lilliputian Land (Splendid China)", a place of fantasy and reality, do come to this street and you will feel as if you placed yourself in a town of southern China, bustling with activity. The name "A Street in Suzhou" is conceived from the style of architecture, but in reality it is the epitome of the traditional downtown streets of the small town in southern China. It has perfectly preserved the artistic features of the culture of China. You will be dazzled by the endless array of beautiful handicraft articles and tourist souvenirs, various famous calligraphies and paintings. Tourists may also watch on-the-spot demonstration of the making of handicraft articles by the craftsmen. There are Beijing, Sichuan, Jiangsu and Cantonese food as well as traditional flavour of delicacies and snacks from various places of the country and your eyes are kept fully occupied.

"A Street in Suzhou" is a comprehensive service area, the shops here can be classified into three kinds. The first type of the shops specially deals in traditional arts and crafts from various places of China and tourist souvenirs with national features. These shops are decorated with antique style in art. They consist of "eight Ge" and "two Yuan", and the logotypes of the shops are written by the celebrated calligraphers, such as "Cang Zhen Ge", "Gu Su Ge", "Zhang An Ge", "Yan Jing Ge", etc. Tourists may buy China's famous potteries and carvings, hand-painted products, wall decorations, palm-woven articles, household utensils and national costumes, etc. The potted landscapes on display in "Ji Jin Yuan" will make you fondle admiringly. Souvenirs with unique characteristics of Splendid China — the lifelike pottery figurines are awaiting your choice in "Ling Long Ju". You may buy Chinese famous wines, drink it on the spot or make a present for your friends and relatives.

The second type of shops engages in China's famous calligraphies and paintings. In "Jin Bao Zhai", you can enjoy the authentic work of calligraphy by the first-class China's calligraphers of modern times and many paintings of famous young and middle-aged painters in China. You will be reluctant to leave the place and feel as if you entered the elegant hall of art. The best quality of "the four treasures of the study" — the writing brush of Wuhu, the ink stick of Anhui, the ink slab of Duanxi and the paper of Jingxuan, and the "Eight Treasures" red ink paste used for seals of Zhangzhou. At your leisure time, you may delight in it or wield your writing brush. This can be very enjoyable for you.

The rest of the buildings are restaurants. Chinese cuisine, with a long history and superb skill, to be close to an art, is one of the component parts of the traditional Chinese culture. In "A Street in Suzhou", there are Beijing, Sichuan, Jiangsu and Cantonese food, with famous chefs in charge and good in colour, fragrance and taste. "Food Street" — "a street in the Street", converges thousands of varied traditional flavour of delicacies and snacks from royal to folk styles, and Chinese-style buffet is available, too. You can have meals at elegant private rooms, rich or thrifty, and the choice is up to you.

When tourists come to visit this ancient, charming "A Street in Suzhou", they will be accorded courteous service and Chinese traditional hospitality.

The 360 Degree Giant-Screen Cinema, located in the southwest of Splendid China, is one of the most modern cinemas in the world at present. It is composed of nine cameras shooting the scenes from various angles, and then nine film projectors showing the picture on the screen synchronously in coordination with the effect of all-round stereo hi-fi set. The scene is so vividly portrayed that you feel as if you were participating in it. The ''Magnificent China at a Glance'' is the first full-length scenery film shown here. By a visit to ''Splendid China'' scenic area, you will travel over a land of charm and beauty in China through the screen.

When you are watching the film, you seem to be drinking in the beauty of Mt. Huangshan. It is now shrouded in mist and clouds, and now covered with a heavy fog. You have just appreciated the beautiful sunset on Kunming Lake, and immediately you are taken by a bus running on the ancient Silk Road in Xinjiang. When you are still immersed in the memories of visiting the relics of the ancient city, the scene suddenly shoots to the sky as if you were taking a helicopter to come to Guilin, a place with the most beautiful scenery under heaven.

You need not take a step, but you may go to southern China to enjoy the picturesque scenery where the breeze is gentle and the sun warm and instantly you come to the north border area to admire a world of ice and snow. You may also experience the life and customs of various national minorities, such as the Kazakhs herding on the snow mountain, the Mongolian herdsmen galloping on the grassland, etc. ''Magnificent China at a Glance'' is a colour, varied, scenery film of 360 degree giant screen. After you have visited ''Splendid China'' miniature scenic spot, you can taste another kind of fresh enjoyment and excitement.

360 Degree Giant-Screen Cinema

Folk Song and Dance Performance

For co-ordinating with the static state of the miniature scenic spot and truly expressing the unique customs of the minority nationalities of China, the arrangements of rich and varied performance of folk song and dance are made in the scenic area of Splendid China. Look, the girls wearing "three-inch shoes" are performing a Manchurian style of "Tiny Step Dance". It seems that tourists were brought into the mysterious Manchurian palace. The vigorous and powerful Mongolian "Go Hunting Dance" makes you feel as if you came to the vast expanse of Eerduosi Grassland where wind was swaying the grass and cattle were seen grazing there. When you listen to the vigorous and melodious beats of small drums, it seems as if you joined the merry "Bumper Harvest Dance" with the Uygur people at the foot of Tianshan Mountains. When you appreciate the "Peacock Dance", "Long Drum Dance", "Reed-pipe Wind Instrument Dance" and "Straw Hat Dance" performed by the very pretty and charming girls of the Dai, Yao, Miao, Bai and Li minority nationalities, it seems that hundreds of flowers in full bloom appeared before your eyes. The opera of "Wang Zhaojun Goes Out to the North of the Great Wall", "Women Generals of the Yang Family", etc. will take you into the moving and tragic history in the past.

The folk song-and-dance performance, in various forms and different styles, is the brilliant pearl in the treasure-house of literature and art of China. The artists and dancers coming from different corners of the country give their splendid performances. They are highly praised and win warm cheer and applause from tourists at home and abroad.

入口處
Entrance

候車亭
Light Bus Stand

急救站
First Aid Station

電話亭　Telephone Booth

小賣部　Buffet

停車場　Car Park

洗手間　Toilet

休息廊　Rest Area

服務點　Service Centre

表演場　Performance Ground

水上餐廳　Overwater Restaurant

Distribution Map
of
Scenic Spots
in
"Splendid China"

N

48 泰山 Mt.Taishan
49 蓬萊閣 Penglai Pavilion
50 圓明園 (紅色虛線範圍內)
    Yuanmingyuan (within the boundary line)
51 崇興寺雙塔
    Twin Pagodas in Chongxing Temple
52 山海關 Shanhaiguan Pass
53 避暑山莊 Imperial Mountain Resorts
54 明十三陵 The Ming Tombs
55 四合院 Quadrangle
56 蘆溝橋 Lugouqiao (Marco Polo Bridge)
57 趙州橋 Zhaozhou Bridge
58 頤和園 The Summer Palace
59 編鐘館 The Hall of Bronze Chime Bells
60 孔廟 Temple of Confucius
61 中山陵 Dr. Sun Yat-sen's Mausoleum
62 天壇 The Temple of Heaven
63 應縣木塔 Yingxian Wooden Pagoda
64 黃帝陵 Huangdi Tomb
65 秦陵兵馬俑
    Terra Cotta Warriors and Horses
    of Qin Shihuang Mausoleum
66 大雁塔 Big Wild Goose Pagoda
67 陝北民居 Cave Houses in Northern Shaanxi
68 金剛寶座塔 Jin Gang Bao Zuo Pagoda
69 妙應寺白塔
    The White Pagoda in Miaoying Temple
70 故宮 The Imperial Palace
71 御花園 Imperial Garden
72 萬里長城 The Great Wall
73 昭君墓 The Tomb of Wang Zhaojun
74 成吉思汗陵 The Mausoleum of Genghis Khan
75 蒙古包 Mongolian Yurt
76 大清真寺 The Id Kah Mosque
77 香妃墓 Xiang Fei's Tomb
78 天山 Tianshan Mountains
79 嘉峪關 Jiayuguan Pass
80 布達拉宮 Potala Palace
81 360度環幕電影院
    360-degree Screen Movie Theatre
82 蘇州街 Suzhou Street

錦繡中華景點名稱
Names of the Scenic Spots in "Splendid China"

1 九龍壁 Nine-Dragon Wall
2 莫高窟 The Mogao Grottoes
3 龍門石窟 The Longmen Grottoes
4 雲岡石窟 The Yungang Grottoes
5 樂山大佛 Leshan Grand Buddha Statue
6 杜甫草堂 Du Fu's Thatched Cottage
7 武侯祠 Memorial Temple of Zhuge Liang
8 長江三峽 Three Gorges of Yangtze River
9 曼飛龍塔 Manfeilong Pagoda
10 白族民居 The Bai Dwelling Houses
11 傣族村寨 The Dai Village
12 大理三塔 Three Ancient Pagodas in Dali
13 石林 The Stone Forest
14 景真八角亭 Jingzhen Octagonal Pavilion
15 漓江山水 Scenery of Li River
16 七星岩 Seven-Star Crags
17 佛山祖廟 Foshan Ancestral Temple
18 西樵山 Xiqiao Mountain
19 五指山、天涯海角
    Five-Finger Mountain "Heaven's Limit and Sea's Margin"
20 媽祖廟 The Temple of Goddess of the Sea
21 客家土樓 The Dwelling House of the Hakkas
22 阿里山、野柳
    Alishan Mountain Scenic Spot Yehliu Park

23 滕王閣 Tengwang Tower
24 黃山 Mt. Huangshan
25 鎮海樓 Zhenhai Tower
26 黃鶴樓 Yellow Crane Tower
27 岳陽樓 The Yueyang Pavilion
28 少林寺 Shaolin Temple
29 塔林 The Pagoda Forest
30 嵩岳寺塔 The Pagoda in Songyue Temple
31 侗族鼓樓和風雨橋
    Wind and Rain Bridge, Drum Tower of the Dong
32 少數民族民居 Dwellings of ethnical groups
33 黃果樹瀑布 Huanguoshu Falls
34 崖墓懸棺 Cliff-Side tombs
35 聖壽寺 Longerity Temple
36 大足石刻 Buddhist Stone Sculpture in Dazu
37 懸空寺 The Midair Temple
38 飛虹塔 Feihong Pagoda
39 晉祠 Jin Ancestral Temple
40 南禪寺 Nanchan Temple
41 古觀星台 Ancient Star-Observatory
42 水鄉小鎮 Water-Village
43 網獅園 Fishermen's Net Garden
44 西湖風光 Scenery of West Lake
45 寒山寺 Hanshan Temple
46 瘦西湖 Slender West Lake
47 城隍廟 The Town God's Temple

123

CHINA TRAVEL SERVICE (HONG KONG) LIMITED

Licence No: 350273

(General Agent for the Business of "Splendid China" in Hong Kong, Macau, Taiwan as well as Overseas)
CTS House, 78-83 Connaught Road Central, Hong Kong.
Tel: 28533888   G.P.O. Box 6016   Telex: 73344 HKCTS HX
Fax: 28541383   Cable Address: Travelbank

SHENZHEN SPECIAL ECONOMIC ZONE OVERSEAS CHINESE TOWN ECONOMIC DEVELOPMENT CO. LTD.

Overseas Chinese Town, Shenzhen Special Economic Zone, China.
TEL: 6600925 6600931 6600248
Telex: 420703 SBH CN
Fax: 6600936   Cable: 3097

SHENZHEN "SPLENDID CHINA" MINIATURE SCENIC SPOT

Publisher: Research & Development Dept.
          China Travel Service (Holdings) Hong Kong Limited
Text By: Liu Chi Ping   Yip Chuen Leung   Tang Jun
         Cheung Yuet Sim   Yiu Lai   Wong Mei
Translated By: Au Lai Wa   Ko Yik Hing
Art By: Wong Shun Kit   Lo Shuk Hing   Sung Pan   Lei Sou Mui
Photographs By: Tse Kwok Kee   Mok Pak Kun   Peng Gao Rui
              Tang Jun   Wong Shun Kit   Wang Yu Fei
Designed & Published By: China Travel Advertising Hong Kong Limited